Business Leaders:
Oprah Winfrey

Bu$ine$$ Leader$
Oprah Winfrey

Judy L. Hasday

MORGAN
REYNOLDS

PUBLISHING

Greensboro, North Carolina

B
WINFREY

Bu$ine$$ Leader$:

Russell Simmons
Steve Jobs
Oprah Winfrey
Warren Buffett
Michael Dell
Ralph Lauren
Faces Behind Beauty

BUSINESS LEADERS: OPRAH WINFREY

Copyright © 2009 By Judy L. Hasday

Library of Congress Cataloging-in-Publication Data

Hasday, Judy L., 1957-
  Business leaders : Oprah Winfrey / by Judy L. Hasday.
     p. cm.
  Includes bibliographical references and index.
  ISBN-13: 978-1-59935-096-7
  ISBN-10: 1-59935-096-3
  1. Winfrey, Oprah. 2. Television personalities--United States--Biography.
3. Actors--United States--Biography. I. Title.
  PN1992.4.W56H37 2008
  384.55092--dc22
  [B]

                                        2008011691

Printed in the United States of America

First Edition

Contents

Oprah Winfrey
(Courtesy of AP Images)

ONE

The Talkingest Child

At the age of three and a half, Oprah Winfrey had a reputation as an amazing public speaker. Taught to read by her grandmother at an early age, the little girl would stand before the congregation of the Buffalo United Methodist Church, in her hometown of Kosciusko, Mississippi, easily reciting stories and speeches. Talking came easily to "Little Mistress Winfrey," as she was called. "[People] would say to my grandmother, 'Hattie Mae, this child sure can talk. She is the talkingest child,'" Winfrey recalled. "I received my sense of value, my sense of esteem, my sense of who I was, my sense of well-being, from speaking out loud."

The talent would lead the young child to keep on talking as an adult, in a career as the host for the highest-rated talk show in television history. Today, dubbed queen of daytime TV, Oprah has a "congregation" of television viewers estimated at 46 million per week. Her words reach around the

A church near Winfrey's birthplace in Kosciusko, Mississippi. *(Courtesy of Witold Skrypczak/Alamy)*

world, as her popular show is broadcast in more than 130 countries. Oprah's successes in entertainment and business have made her the first African American woman billionaire. But she is also a committed philanthropist, often described as one of the world's most influential people.

The woman who wields such wealth and power today came from a humble background. Oprah Gail Winfrey was born to an unwed mother on January 29, 1954, in the small Mississippi town of Kosciusko. Located about seventy miles northeast of the state capital of Jackson, the town is named after Tadeusz Kosciuszko, a Polish general who assisted the colonists in their struggle for independence during the Revolutionary War.

Oprah is the great-great granddaughter of slaves who lived in the Loess Hills region of Mississippi in the mid-1800s. Constantine and Violet belonged to white landowner Absalom Winfrey and his wife Sarah Lucinda. At the outbreak of the Civil War in 1861 Absalom went off to war, leaving Sarah, Constantine, and Violet to care for the farm in his absence. At war's end, Absalom returned home and gave Constantine and Violet their freedom. Already married, they took on Absalom's last name.

In 1876, Constantine Winfrey made an agreement with a local landowner named John Watson. In exchange for picking eighty bales of cotton, each weighing four hundred pounds (for a total of 32,000 pounds) within a certain period of time, Watson would give Constantine eighty acres of land. In 1881, Constantine obtained the property. Subsequent generations of the Winfrey family remained in the area, many of them making a living as farmers.

During the 1950s, one of Constantine's great-grandsons was a soldier based at Fort Rucker Army post in Dale County, Alabama. While on leave in May 1953, Vernon Winfrey had a chance romantic encounter with Vernita Lee, whose family lived on a small farm outside Kosciusko. Nine months later, the nineteen-year-old Lee gave birth to a daughter.

Vernita named the child Orpah, after a woman in the Bible's Book of Ruth. However, family friends and relatives had trouble pronouncing the baby's name. They would transpose the "r" and the "p," calling the little girl Oprah.

Vernita and Oprah lived with Vernita's parents, Hattie Mae and Earlist Lee. Oprah's father, Vernon, didn't even know

Winfrey standing with her father, Vernon, in 2003. *(Courtesy of Adriane Jaeckle/Getty Images)*

that he had a child until he received a newspaper clipping announcing the birth. At the time, Oprah's mother included a note asking him to send clothes for the newborn.

In the rural poverty of the South, Vernita had few prospects for work. Hoping to better her life, she headed north in search of a job in Milwaukee, Wisconsin. During the 1950s and 1960s, many blacks had migrated from the rural south to the northern cities in search of work and better pay. Before Oprah's first birthday, the young mother left Oprah in the care of her parents. Oprah soon came to refer to Hattie Mae as "momma," but she tried to stay out of the way of Earlist, who would hurl things at her and chase her away with a cane in hand.

The Lees lived on a farm of just a few acres, and it yielded most of the produce the family ate. The house had no indoor plumbing, no television, or other modern amenities. The bathroom was an outhouse in the yard. Oprah had no bedroom of her own—she slept in a bed with Hattie Mae. The clothes on her back were sewn by her grandmother, and the young girl often went barefoot while doing her chores. She helped out by bringing fresh water from the well into the house, feeding the pigs and chickens, and leading the cow out to the pasture to graze.

A highlight of life for young Oprah was when she stood before the congregation of her grandmother's church. She had memorized many passages from the Bible, and she loved to perform in front of whoever would listen to her.

> I started out speaking there [at the church], and it was a way of getting love. And you know, the sisters sitting in the front row would fan themselves and nod to my grandmother, Hattie Mae. And they'd say, 'Hattie Mae, this child is gifted.' And somehow,

with no education, my grandmother instilled in me a belief that
I could aspire to do great things in my life.

Years later Oprah would credit her grandmother with
instilling in her the importance of education. "My grandmother really raised me to be who I am because of her belief
in education," Oprah says. "Even though she wasn't very
educated, never finished high school, she was strong."

When Oprah was six years old, Vernita sent for her daughter to join her in Milwaukee. In 1960, Oprah left Kosciusko
and moved north to live with a mother she did not know and
a world that was unfamiliar. "I had no relationship or memory
of my mother whatsoever . . . all of a sudden just one day I'm
packed up and put in a car and told, 'You're gonna go live
with your mother now.' It was horrible," she remembered.

Milwaukee in the early 1960s was a bustling industrial
city. Vernita had moved there in hope of obtaining work in a
factory, but many blacks who migrated north to industrial
cities found it difficult to get this kind of work. Vernita
eventually got a job as a maid, and also collected welfare.

Oprah moved in with her mother and Patricia, her one-
year-old half sister (Vernita had given birth to another child
out of wedlock). They were living in a boardinghouse in a
poor, run-down area of Milwaukee, around the Ninth Street
area. The landlady was a light-skinned black woman who,
Oprah later recalled, did not like dark-skinned children. "I
instantly knew that Miss Miller did not like me because of the
color of my skin. I was too dark and I was a nappy-headed
colored child, and Miss Miller would say it."

Making things tougher, Vernita didn't treat the girls
equally. While lighter-skinned Patricia shared a bed in the

house with Vernita, Oprah was left to sleep on a tiny cot in an enclosed porch.

Vernita worked long hours. When she came home she was either too exhausted to spend time with her kids, or she was visiting with various people who happened to flow in and out of the small, one-room apartment. Vernita enrolled six-year-old Oprah in kindergarten at the local school. But because Oprah was already very accomplished in reading and writing, she soon became bored. She wanted to let her kindergarten teacher know how she felt, so Oprah wrote a letter using the biggest words she knew: "Dear Miss Newe, I do not belong here, because I can read and I know a lot of big words: *elephant, hippopotamus.*" Oprah was moved to the first grade the next day. She would later skip second grade, as well.

By 1962, Vernita realized that taking care of two children was more than she could manage. So for the second time in two years, Oprah was shuttled off to live in yet another new home—this time with her father, Vernon, and his wife, Zelma.

After his discharge from the army in 1955, Vernon Winfrey had also moved north, leaving Kosciusko and settling in Nashville, Tennessee. Vernon initially worked as a janitor at Vanderbilt University, but he also attended a trade school. By the late 1950s Vernon owned his own barbershop business. He and Zelma, who had no children of their own, were willing to provide a home for Oprah.

The change in environment was good for eight-year-old Oprah. Vernon and Zelma did not display outward affection to her, she would later say; however, she knew they cared about her well-being. The Winfreys were strong advocates of both spiritual and academic education. Spiritual education came every Sunday when the family attended services at the neighborhood Baptist church, where Vernon served as a deacon. Academic instruction took place in the home as well as at school: Zelma insisted that Oprah read a book every two weeks and write a report. She was also tested on her multiplication tables and had a list of new vocabulary words to learn every week.

In East Nashville, Oprah attended third and fourth grades at Wharton Elementary School. There, she was greatly influenced by her fourth-grade teacher, Mary Duncan. Duncan recognized Oprah's passion for learning and often provided extra encouragement and praise for her young student. Oprah would later say of her teacher, "She so believed in me, and for the first time, made me embrace the idea of learning. I learned to love learning because of Mrs. Duncan."

Oprah flourished in the safe, structured environment provided by Vernon and Zelma. However, the summer after fourth grade, Vernita contacted Vernon and told him she wanted Oprah to come back to Milwaukee. She had moved into a two-room apartment and had plans for a better future. "Come live with me," Vernita told her nine-year-old daughter. "I'm gonna get married and we're all gonna be a real family."

For the next six years, Oprah shuttled back and forth between her mother in Milwaukee and father in Nashville. "That whole part of my life," she explained, "was about going back and forth from one parent to the next. So I never developed deep roots or connections to either parent."

When Oprah arrived in Milwaukee, she discovered that living with her mother was not very different from what it had been before. Vernita's two-room apartment was just as cramped, because Oprah now had to share the space not only with her mother and sister, Patricia, but also her mother's live-in boyfriend and a new little brother, named Jeffrey. Vernita continued to work long hours, leaving Oprah to care for Patricia and Jeffrey during the day. The apartment was also a stopover for friends and relatives who drifted in and out of Milwaukee.

One of those relatives, a nineteen-year-old male cousin, sexually assaulted Oprah when she was just nine years old. Confused and frightened by the rape, she told no one what had happened. "I didn't tell anybody about it because I thought I would be blamed for it," Oprah later explained. "I remember blaming myself for it, thinking something must be wrong with me."

The sexual abuse, by another cousin's boyfriend and an uncle, would continue for many years. Oprah buried her feelings somewhere deep inside of her. However, she would later admit that being abused led to her becoming, in her own words, "a sexually promiscuous teenager."

Despite her personal trauma, Oprah continued to excel academically in school. One of the teachers at her middle school recommended that she attend the Upward Bound program. This national program had been created to provide greater educational opportunities for disadvantaged students by allowing them to attend schools in better neighborhoods. After being accepted into the program, thirteen-year-old Oprah was enrolled in Nicolet High, a public school located in the Milwaukee suburban community of Glendale. Despite being the only black child in the student body, she quickly made friends with many of her classmates.

Although Oprah thrived academically in her new environment, she was feeling conflicted. As she traveled each day outside her poverty-stricken neighborhood, Oprah saw how other, wealthier people lived.

> The life that I saw those children lead was so totally different from what I went home to, from what I saw when I took the bus home with the maids in the evening. I wanted my mother to be like their mothers. I wanted my mother to have cookies ready for me when I came home and to say, "How was your day?" But she was one of those maids. And she was tired. And she was just trying to survive. Her way of showing love to me was getting out and going to work every day, putting clothes on my back, and having food on the table. At that time, I didn't understand that.

Oprah stole money from her mother to buy things, go to the movies, or just hang out with her new friends. She often lied about where she had been and what she had been doing. She would stay out late at nights, and by age fourteen she was living on the streets and out of control. Realizing that she could not handle her daughter, Vernita looked into placing Oprah in a home for troubled teens. But the juvenile hall was at capacity, so Vernita placed a call to Nashville asking Vernon to take his daughter into his home again.

Vernon and Zelma agreed, and in 1968 Oprah moved to Nashville. Vernon and Zelma made it very clear to Oprah what the rules were in their household. If she was going to live with them, she would have to abide by those rules—all of them. Vernon told Oprah that she would have to concentrate on her education, dress appropriately, be respectful, and be home by curfew.

Vernon and Zelma did not know that fourteen-year-old Oprah was hiding the secret of being pregnant. "I was so ashamed, I hid the pregnancy until my swollen ankles and belly gave me away," Oprah wrote later. A few months after returning to Nashville, Oprah gave birth to a boy. But the baby was premature and died within a few weeks.

Oprah had already been enrolled at East Nashville High School and following the death of her baby, she returned to classes. "I went back to school," she told an interviewer, "and not a soul knew. Nobody." Her father remained supportive, telling Oprah it was time to move forward, to continue her schooling and make something of her life. "What you have done is the past," he told her, "and you alone get to determine what your future will be." So she focused on her schoolwork, and soon showed she could excel academically.

Always a voracious reader, Oprah steeped herself in books on African Americans, particularly those about women. She familiarized herself with the stories of women born into slavery, such as Harriet Tubman and Sojourner Truth, who despite many struggles went on to achieve great things. For Oprah, learning about her roots and her black heritage was an important part of her self-education. She felt inspired by the strength and determination of these women of color.

A contemporary novel that struck a chord with Oprah was an autobiographical book published in 1970 by a woman named Maya Angelou (Marguerite Johnson). An African American woman who, like Oprah, had been born in the South, Angelou had dealt with a painful past of sexual abuse, which she detailed in her novel, *I Know Why the Caged Bird Sings*. Oprah later recalled how she felt after reading the book as a teenager: "That was the first time I thought, there

Harriet Tubman *(Library of Congress)*

is a story about me! And it said to me that my life and what happened in my life mattered." Oprah would not speak about her abuse for many more years.

While in high school, Oprah made many friends. She participated in extra-curricular activities, including drama club and forensics speech (debate club), where she excelled as a public speaker. As part of her recitation repertoire, she memorized two favorite writers' works—*Jubilee,* a novel by Margaret Walker, and "Ain't I a Woman," a speech by Sojourner Truth. Oprah soon became known around Nashville for her powerful oratory skills and was often invited to speak before various civic groups.

Within the Nashville church community, Oprah was known for organizing and participating in presentations of *God's Trombones: Seven Negro Sermons in Verse,* a series of poetic sermons written by African American lawyer and educator James Weldon Johnson (1871-1938). "I used to do them for churches all over the city of Nashville," Oprah said. "I've spoken at every church in Nashville at some point in my life. You sort of get known for that. Other people were known for singing; I was known for talking."

In April 1971, Oprah was one of 1,400 delegates to the White House Conference on Youth held in Estes Park, Colorado. Approximately five hundred adults from fields such as education, business, media, and religion attended the event, along with 918 youth delegates. Two students from each state, as well as from various countries around the world, were invited to join business leaders in dialogues on topics such as the environment, drug use, legal rights and justice, and poverty. Oprah was one of the students selected to represent Tennessee.

I Sell the Shadow to Support the Substance.

SOJOURNER TRUTH.

James Weldon Johnson *(Library of Congress)*

Upon her return from the conference, Oprah was interviewed at a local radio station, Nashville's WVOL. Station deejay John Heidelberg had met Oprah earlier in the year when she had solicited his sponsorship in a fundraiser for the March of Dimes Walkathon. Heidelberg made a tape record-

Maya Angelou posing with her book, *I Know Why the Caged Bird Sings*, in 1971. *(Courtesy of AP Images)*

ing of Oprah reading some copy and shared it with his station manager, Clarence Kilcrese. Like Heidelberg, Kilcrese was impressed with Oprah's speaking ability and had her come back to formally audition for a job with the radio station.

At the age of seventeen, Oprah was hired to read the news for WVOL on the weekends and after school during the week. The job paid well for a high school student—$100.00 a week. Oprah explained, "I had to work after school. I'd finish, get there by 3:30, and I'd do on-the-air newscasts. Well, all my friends just hated me because they were cutting grass." In addition to juggling the job with her schoolwork, Oprah made time for other school activities. She was elected vice-president of the student council and selected to the Honor Society.

Another opportunity for Oprah occurred when she represented WVOL Radio in a Miss Fire Prevention contest. Each contestant was asked what she wanted to do with her life. When Oprah's turn came, she replied that she wanted to be a broadcast journalist. She recalls, "I made this big speech about broadcast journalism—mainly because I had seen Barbara Walters that morning on *The Today Show*," she notes. "I said I wanted to be a broadcast journalist because I believed in the truth. I was interested in proclaiming the truth to the world and all. And I won the contest." Oprah became the first black woman in Nashville to be crowned Miss Fire Prevention.

Oprah went on to compete in other pageants that year. She was named Miss Black Tennessee, which earned her a partial college scholarship. As Miss Black Tennessee, Oprah then competed in the Miss Black America pageant in 1971, although she did not win.

After graduating from East Nashville High, Oprah was ready to go to college. Vernon supported the idea of his daughter furthering her education, but he did not want her to live away from home. So, in the fall of 1971 Oprah enrolled as a commuter student at Tennessee State University (TSU), an all-black college in Nashville. Because the university did not offer courses of study in radio and television at the undergraduate level, however, she chose to major in speech and drama.

TWO

"This is What I Should Have Been Doing"

During the early 1970s, many businesses were responding to the U.S. presidential executive order of the mid-1960s requiring businesses to take "affirmative action" toward hiring minority employees.

In Nashville, television station WLAC was looking to hire minority employees. Few women were in television news broadcasting at the time, so as an African American and a woman Oprah Winfrey represented two minorities. A station manager approached her while she was in her sophomore year in college, asking her to interview for a job with WLAC-TV. She admitted to feeling anxious about the job. "I'd never even been behind the scenes in television," she explained. "I was nineteen at the time."

To succeed with the interview, Winfrey thought she should emulate the well-known *Today Show* news reporter, Barbara

Walters. "So I decided to pretend to be Barbara Walters because that's how I'd gotten into this in the first place. So I sat there, pretending, with Barbara in my head. Did everything I thought she would do. And I was hired. It's amazing." The new weekend co-anchor on Nashville's Channel 5 WLAC-TV was Nashville's first female and first black TV-news anchor. A $15,000-a-year salary went with the job.

Winfrey now had to juggle her college schoolwork with a full-time job. She explained, "So I'd do all my classes in the morning, from eight o'clock to one o'clock, and in the afternoon, I'd work from two o'clock to ten o'clock and did the six o'clock news. And I would stay up and study and all that until one, two, three o'clock in the morning, and then just start the routine all over again." The busy schedule left little time for other college activities, but Winfrey's focus was a career in television. She was soon promoted from the weekend co-anchor position to weeknight co-anchor, serving alongside seasoned newscaster Harry Chapman. Winfrey spent her sophomore, junior, and part of her senior years working at WLAC, which changed its name in 1975 to WTVF-TV.

In 1976, when Winfrey was just shy of completing her senior project in order to graduate from TSU, she was contacted by a television station located in Baltimore, Maryland, some six hundred miles away. WJZ-TV, an American Broadcasting Company (ABC) affiliate was looking for some new on-air talent to host the six o'clock news. The station already had a veteran anchor, Jerry Turner. However, management planned to expand the news program from thirty minutes to an hour and wanted two anchors presenting the news.

Although Oprah recognized that the Baltimore job was a great opportunity, accepting the position would require her

Barbara Walters on the set of *The Today Show* in 1965. *(Courtesy of AP Images)*

to leave her college education unfinished. Still, because the job was in a larger broadcast market, compared to Nashville, she would be gaining the chance to make her mark in the "big leagues" of broadcasting.

Hired at a salary of $22,000 per year, twenty-two-year-old Oprah Winfrey settled into her job as news co-anchor in Baltimore. But things did not go well. As a reporter, she was criticized for lacking the necessary detachment in covering a story. She would have an emotional reaction and cry when a story was sad, she explained:

> I used to go on assignment and be so open that I would say to people at fires—and they've lost their children—'That's okay. You don't have to talk to me.' Well, then you go back to the newsroom, and the news director says, 'What do you mean they didn't have to talk to you?' I'd say, 'But she just lost her child, and you know I just felt so bad.'

Within a year she was on her way out the door.

> I only came to co-host a talk show because I had failed at news and I was going to be fired. . . . So when I was called in and put on the edge of being fired and certainly demoted and knew that firing was only a couple weeks away, I was devastated. I was twenty-two and embarrassed by the whole thing because I had never failed before.

Fortunately, she had signed a contract, so the station did not want to fire her. She explains, "Because they had no place else to put me, they put me on a talk show in the morning."

The talk show format had been pioneered by Phil Donahue, who in the late 1960s moved his popular radio talk show

Phil Donahue speaks with an audience member on the set of his show in 1985. *(Courtesy of Yvonne Hemsey/Getty Images)*

program, based in Dayton, Ohio, to television. Donahue has been credited with inventing the successful television talk show format, in which the host, holding a microphone, moves among members of the audience, asking questions and taking comments. This technique makes the audience become part of the performance. Donahue understood how the relationship between host and listener worked—there had to be a connection made between the two in order for viewers to stay interested.

In the 1960s, daytime talk shows targeted females, who made up much of the viewing audience. At that time, there were more stay-at-home women than men. Although Phil Donahue tailored his television talk show to women, he moved beyond the cooking tips and fashion wear features that were typical of the morning television show circuit, and presented more serious—and often controversial—topics. Donahue would leave the stage and go down into the audience to discuss a show's topic with its members. Television viewers loved this new talk show format.

In 1970, *The Phil Donahue Show* was syndicated—syndication refers to when individual television stations purchase the rights to broadcast a show. Almost overnight *The Phil Donahue Show* became a huge hit, rising to number one in its time slot nationally. In 1974, Donahue relocated his show to Chicago, Illinois, and it was renamed simply *Donahue*.

WJZ-TV management wanted to make a talk show to compete locally in Baltimore against nationally syndicated *Donahue*. It was thought that Oprah Winfrey could serve as a co-host, along with reporter Richard Sher, for the new magazine-style talk show, called *People Are Talking*. It was first broadcast on April 14, 1978.

Winfrey's freewheeling conversational style—the very same style that didn't work for news reporting—worked like a charm in the informal talk show format. After she finished the first show, Winfrey immediately knew she had found her niche.

> And I'm telling you, the hour I interviewed—my very first interview was the Carvel Ice Cream Man, and Benny from *All My Children*—I'll never forget it. I came off the air, thinking, 'This is what I should have been doing.' Because it was like breathing to me, like breathing. You just talk. 'Be yourself' is really what I had learned to do.

Because she was relaxed and able to be herself while on air, Winfrey proved to be very successful as a talk show host. She changed the information focus format of the Phil Donahue talk show to a more personal one. Instead of experts on issues, ordinary people would share something about themselves. And with her vibrant personality and gift for getting people to talk, Winfrey appealed to many viewers. She would ask questions and respond to answers as a good friend would. Winfrey established a rapport with guests on the show and engaged the audience, asking follow-up questions that would probe deeper into the issue being discussed. Vital to her success and appeal, the caring involvement that she conveyed during the program made Winfrey seem like a friend, someone the viewer wanted to share their time with.

Winfrey also shared herself, making her audience familiar with her hopes and failures, as well as her stories about her private life: her poverty as a child, problems with dating, and struggles with losing weight. By the early 1980s, Winfrey no longer had her beauty queen figure, but had put on enough weight to be considered somewhat heavyset. But she would be open about herself and make the audience members feel they knew her. That sense of familiarity helped make her talk show very popular.

In Baltimore, the ratings for *People Are Talking* quickly passed those for *The Phil Donahue Show*. *People Are Talking* was a huge success, for WJZ-TV and Winfrey. For the next six years, she would co-host the program. During that time, she polished her skills as a talk show host, and enjoyed her own professional growth. As other talk shows appeared, Winfrey adapted to keep up with the competition.

To prevent host and audience fatigue (doing the same types of shows over and over), Oprah sought out interesting guests who would bring just the slightest edge to the feel of *People Are Talking*. At the same time, she worked to introduce topics that she and the audience would find stimulating. Winfrey infused controversial topics to keep the audience actively engaged but not uncomfortable. Betrayal in a marriage, abortion, and suicide were among the more "hot button" topics. The ratings typically rose higher and higher as more of these kinds of shows aired.

In 1983, after five years on *People Are Talking*, Winfrey began to feel that she had progressed as far as she could as co-host on the WJZ-TV show. Although she knew that she wanted to move to a bigger television market, she was not sure where she should go. But Winfrey did believe that she needed to make a career move: "When you have finished growing in one place or time, you know. Your soul tells you when it's time to move on."

Debra DiMaio, a former producer for *People Are Talking*, had already moved on. She had taken a position as executive producer at WLS-TV Chicago, an ABC affiliate. That station was looking for a way to boost its ratings for its morning show *A.M. Chicago*. Since its move to Chicago in 1974, *Donahue* had been dominating the airwaves on competing station WGN-TV. By 1983, *A.M. Chicago*'s ratings in the morning show time slot had plummeted to third place, and its host, Robb Weller, had quit. DiMaio was responsible for producing a talk show that was in the bottom of the ratings and had no host.

In an effort to fill the empty position, DiMaio showed a demo tape of *People Are Talking* to WLS-TV vice president

Debra DiMaio *(Courtesy of Kevin Horan/Time Life Pictures/Getty Images)*

and general manager Dennis Swanson. The tape contained segments featuring co-hosts Richard Sher and Oprah Winfrey. Swanson was wowed by what he saw in Winfrey. After he learned that *People Are Talking* was beating *Donahue* in the television ratings in Baltimore, Swanson was sold on bringing her to Chicago to interview for the host spot.

Despite concerns that she was too heavy, the wrong gender, and the wrong color to be welcome in Chicago, Winfrey agreed to meet with Swanson and DiMaio. Several people advised her that the move to Chicago would never work, but her best friend, Gayle King, was not among them. King, who had known Winfrey since 1976, was a production assistant at WJZ-TV Baltimore. Upon hearing about the open position, she told Winfrey, "You should go to Chicago! You can beat Donahue—I know you can."

Winfrey followed her friend's advice and went for the interview. Upon arriving in Chicago, she was delighted. "I'll tell you this," she later recalled. "My first day in Chicago, September fourth, 1983, I set foot in this city, and just walking down the street, it was like roots, like the motherland. I knew I belonged here."

To audition for the job, Winfrey was required to give a mock interview. The enthusiasm, energy, and on-camera ease she brought to that performance convinced Swanson. He offered her a four-year contract, at a starting salary of $230,000 a year, to serve as the sole host of *A.M. Chicago*. After accepting the job, she went back to Baltimore to finish out her contract with WJZ-TV. Oprah Winfrey's last day with the station was December 18, 1983.

Winfrey and her best friend, Gayle King *(Courtesy of Mathew Imaging/FilmMagic)*

THREE

"The Oprah Winfrey Show"

A natural port city and transportation hub in the midwestern United States, Chicago is situated on the southeastern shore of Lake Michigan. In 1980, according to population records from the U. S. Bureau of the Census, more than 3 million people lived in Chicago, making it the second-largest city in the United States. It was much larger than Baltimore, which, with a population of about 786,000, ranked tenth. Chicago had a vibrant downtown area, served by a mass transit system that encircled the downtown business district.

Oprah Winfrey began her new job at the ABC-7 studio on North State Street—a major thoroughfare that runs through the heart of downtown Chicago. Soon after arriving in the city, on Monday, January 2, 1984, she hosted her first *A.M. Chicago* program. Winfrey made the most of the thirty-minute show, which centered on the topic of How to Marry the Man or Woman of Your Choice.

To prepare for her role as host of *A.M. Chicago*, Winfrey researched information about some of the program's former hosts and their approaches in conducting the show. In planning for the shows, she made sure to prepare herself with information on scheduled guests, reading up on them the night before their appearance on the show so she could get a feel for their personality, understand their viewpoints on controversial topics, and learn enough about them to carry on a conversational style interview.

Winfrey related easily to her audiences. Her sincere, concerned, and empathetic personality came across to her viewers, who would say that she seemed like one of them. Many said that Oprah Winfrey was the kind of person who understood the kinds of everyday difficulties most average people deal with.

Winfrey in her *A.M. Chicago* office in 1985. *(Courtesy of AP Images/Charlie Knoblock)*

Another characteristic of Winfrey that contributed to her early success was her ability to be comfortable with stepping outside the classic interviewer role. If her feet hurt from being in her high-heeled shoes too long, Winfrey thought nothing of flipping them off during the show. Such everyday kind of behavior appealed to many viewers.

As she had done on *People Are Talking*, Winfrey brought controversial and sometimes uncomfortable topics to her Chicago talk show. Topics would include hate crimes, incest, anorexia, child abuse, and sexual abuse. She also interviewed a variety of guests on the show, including celebrities such as actresses Shirley MacLaine and Goldie Hawn; entertainers Stevie Wonder and Paul McCartney; and even her idols, Barbara Walters and Maya Angelou.

WLS-TV ran *A.M. Chicago* at the same time as *Donahue*, and within four weeks of being on the air, Winfrey's new show went from last place in its time slot to number one. Four months later, the station extended the show, making it an hour-long program. Within six months, Winfrey had more than twice the number of viewers tuning in to her show than were watching *Donahue*. By the end of 1984, *Newsweek* magazine had named Oprah Winfrey the hottest media star in Chicago.

In an article describing Winfrey and her early success on the talk show scene, *Time* magazine described why she rose so quickly:

> What [Winfrey] lacks in journalistic toughness . . . she makes up in plainspoken curiosity, robust humor and, above all, empathy. Guests with sad stories to tell are apt to rouse a tear in Oprah's eye or get a comforting arm around the shoulder. They, in turn, often find themselves revealing things they would not imagine telling anyone, much less a national TV audience.

In 1985, Phil Donahue moved his show from Chicago to New York. He said the move was so he could be closer to his wife, actress Marlo Thomas, who was performing on Broadway. Some people believed Donahue left Chicago because Winfrey had overtaken his show in the ratings. Whatever the reason, with Donahue's departure, she reigned over Chicago's talk show market.

When *A.M. Chicago* was expanded to one hour, Winfrey was given more hands-on control of the show. She could make decisions on what guests to have on the program and on the topics to be discussed. In September 1985, the show was renamed *The Oprah Winfrey Show.*

That year, while in Chicago on business, producer and multiple Grammy Award-winner Quincy Jones tuned in to Oprah's show one morning in his hotel room. Back home in Los Angeles, Jones had been working on coproducing a film adaptation of *The Color Purple,* the 1982 novel by Alice Walker. The story, which takes place in the rural South of the 1930s, centers on a poor black girl struggling to overcome a life of abuse and poverty.

In addition to writing the musical score for the film, Jones was working with director Steven Spielberg to bring the Pulitzer Prize–winning novel to the big screen. The decision to have Spielberg direct the movie had been con- troversial. Many blacks in the film industry questioned why a white director had been hired for a project about a black experience. In response, Quincy Jones had been brought in as a coproducer.

Jones had formulated in his mind how certain charac- ters should look. And when he looked at Oprah Winfrey on television, he saw not the talk show host, but Sofia, the steely, independent-minded character in Walker's novel. Jones called the film's casting company, Reuben Cannon and Associates, and requested that Winfrey be invited to audition for the part.

When Winfrey got the call, she was ecstatic. She had read *The Color Purple* while still living in Baltimore and fallen in love with the novel. The opportunity to act in a film adaptation of the novel was one she had already dreamed of, she told an interviewer:

> I thought of *The Color Purple* for myself. . . . I read the book. I got so many copies of that book. I passed the book around to everybody I knew. If I was on a bus, I'd pass it out to people. And when I heard that there was going to be a movie, I started talking it up for myself. I didn't know Quincy Jones or Steven Spielberg, or how on earth I would get in this movie. I'd never acted in my life. But I felt it so intensely that I had to be a part of that movie. I really do believe that I created it for myself. I wanted it more than anything in the world, and would have done anything to do it, anything to do it.

When she read the book, Winfrey had instantly connected to Sofia. The character is a strong woman who, after being mistreated and abused by men, eventually loses her spirit and ability to fight. Winfrey's own history of sexual abuse was not public knowledge at the time. In the 1980s, she had yet to tell anyone outside her family about how she had been sexually abused as a child, but it remained a part of her.

In auditioning for the part of Sofia, Winfrey worked with Willard Pugh, who played the part of Sofia's husband, Harpo. The screen test went well and Spielberg offered Winfrey the part. When she heard that news, she declared it was "the single happiest day in my life."

Winfrey in a scene from the movie *The Color Purple* *(Courtesy of Photos 12/Alamy)*

Winfrey had long dreamed of the opportunity of becoming an actress. While working in Baltimore, she had thought about quitting her job as a television newswoman to pursue an acting career. She explained, "I felt at the time, I can't quit this job because this is what everybody else wants to do. And if I quit this job, what am I doing to do?" So she figured in order for her to become an actress, she would have to be discovered. Winfrey told a friend of the plan: "[S]he said, 'You just dream. You are a dreamer.' So when it happened I called her up. I said, 'You will not believe this! I got discovered!'"

Winfrey in 1986
(Courtesy of AP Images/
Douglas C. Pizac)

To take the role, Oprah had to juggle her film schedule around the schedule for the taping of her show. Complications would occur and at one point, Oprah was prepared to quit the talk show altogether. Finally, an arrangement was worked out in which she was allowed to take off eight weeks from the show. In her absence, guest hosts filled in and popular reruns were aired.

The Color Purple premiered in New York City on December 16, 1985, and in Los Angeles two days later. The story is harsh and portrays several black male characters as abusive and cruel. Some members of the black community were offended by the negative portrayal, and they picketed several theaters showing the film. In response, Winfrey raised what she felt was a more relevant issue—the plight of women who are victims of abuse. "Let's talk about the issue of wife abuse, violence against women, sexual abuse of children in the home," Winfrey said at the time. Defending Walker's novel, she said, "What the book did for me, and what the movie is doing for other women who were sexually abused, is pointing up that you're not the only one."

Despite the controversy, *The Color Purple* received numerous award nominations in 1986. Among them were eleven Academy Award nominations, including Best Actress for Whoopi Goldberg and a Best Supporting Actress nod for Winfrey. Ultimately, the film did not win a single Oscar, though Winfrey did win a Golden Globe Award. However, several of the film's stars as well as director Spielberg had left an indelible imprint on the entertainment industry in bringing Walker's story to the big screen.

With her success as an actress and in her talk show, Winfrey was earning a great deal of money. At the end of 1985, she decided to share some of her wealth with others. When she learned that the management at WLS-TV had decided not to give seven of her vital staff members an end-of-year bonus, Winfrey took care of them herself by writing them each a $10,000 check from her personal account.

Fame had come quickly to Winfrey, who in the mid-1980s was receiving national attention and recognition for her work in both the television and the film industries. At the same time, Winfrey was setting her sights on bigger and better things—and on taking more control of her life.

FOUR

"You Could Own Your Own Show"

"I intend to do and have it all," Winfrey told an interviewer in the 1980s. "I want to have a movie career, a television career, a talk-show career. I will continue to be fulfilled doing all these things, because no one can tell me how to live my life. I believe in my own possibilities, and I feel I can do it all."

Because she wanted more control over the film and television projects that she worked on, Winfrey decided to form her own production company. August 1986 saw the establishment of Harpo Productions, Inc., with Oprah serving as producer, chief executive officer, and chairman. (Harpo is Oprah spelled backwards; it is also the name of Sophia's husband in *The Color Purple*.) Winfrey gave a 5 percent share of her new company to her lawyer and manager Jeffrey Jacobs, who would later serve as the production company's president and chief operating officer, or COO.

Earlier in 1985, Jacobs had worked out a deal with the television program syndicator King World Productions to take over production of *The Oprah Winfrey Show*. But more important, King World would also offer *The Oprah Winfrey Show* for syndication to hundreds of individual ABC-network affiliated television stations that were broadcasting all over the country.

One of the executives with King World Productions, the late Roger King, has been credited with helping to turn Oprah Winfrey's talk show in Chicago into a national phenomenon. Because he had already had success with syndicating shows suxh as *Jeopardy* and *Wheel of Fortune*, King was able to convince many station managers to buy *The Oprah Winfrey*

Roger King (left), Winfrey, and then-WLS-TV station manager Joseph Ahern at a news conference held to announce the syndication of *The Oprah Winfrey Show*. *(Courtesy of AP Images/Charlie Bennet)*

Show. Years later, a friend of King's, Robert V. Madden, would explain that King really believed in Winfrey, telling the heads of the affiliates, "[Winfrey is] quality, she's got a quality show and she's beating Phil Donahue in Chicago."

The arrangement with King World, as negotiated by Jeffrey Jacobs, also allowed Winfrey greater control over the production of *The Oprah Winfrey Show.* Winfrey could make the decisions affecting what would air and when she could be away from taping. She also gained a piece of the financial terms of syndication: Jacobs ensured that Winfrey would obtain 25 percent of the gross that King World made from syndication sales.

By September 1986, approximately 180 local stations had signed on to air *The Oprah Winfrey Show,* and on September 8 the newly syndicated show officially launched. It did not take long for King World to recoup its investment. Within three months, the ratings of *The Oprah Winfrey Show* reflected the show's success. Since it cost less than $100,000 per week to produce the program, the company's profits were significant, bringing in about $30 million by the end of 1986. With her 25 percent share of the syndication revenues of her show, Winfrey earned a staggering $7.5 million in 1986.

King World Productions continued to sell *The Oprah Winfrey Show* in syndication one television station at a time, slowly increasing the number of stations and locations airing the program around the country. Taking the show national placed Winfrey in the living rooms of millions of viewers across the United States. She had already become a celebrity on the streets around Chicago; by the end of 1986 her celebrity reached across the country.

That fame soon brought Winfrey an appearance on the magazine show *60 Minutes*, where she talked about *The Oprah Winfrey Show* with news correspondent Mike Wallace. After Wallace described Winfrey as a "colorful, controversial, and soaring sudden success," she responded that the reason she could communicate so well with her audiences was simply because she was just like them. People were instantly at ease with her because she was just like other folks. Because of her show, however, she had a national forum in which to bring various concerns and issues to everybody.

Some people who did not watch the television show were learning about Winfrey from seeing her in feature films. After the success of *The Color Purple*, Winfrey appeared in another movie, a film adaptation of Richard Wright's novel *Native Son,* directed by Jerrold Freedman. Released in December 1986, the movie depicts the impoverished world of African Americans in 1930s Chicago. Oprah took the role of the mother of the nineteen-year-old protagonist, Bigger Thomas, played by Victor Love. Although reviews of the movie were positive, it did not do well at the box office.

Much more success for Winfrey resulted from her talk show, which continued to do well nationally. In less than a year, *The Oprah Winfrey Show* had become the number one talk show in syndication. Twelve months after its launch as a syndicated program, it showed a profit of $125 million. Oprah's 25 percent cut translated to $31 million dollars, a huge increase from the $230,000-per-year salary she had received while under contract to WLS-TV.

Along with the financial success came recognition from the television industry. In its first year of eligibility, *The Oprah Winfrey Show* won three Daytime Emmy Awards, which are

Winfrey holding her Daytime Emmy award in 1987. *(Courtesy of AP Images)*

honors given for outstanding achievements in television. In June 1987, Oprah's program swept the talk show categories, receiving Emmy Awards for Outstanding Talk or Service Show Host, Outstanding Talk or Service Program, and Outstanding Direction. Many more Daytime Emmy awards would follow in the coming years.

A year after *The Oprah Winfrey Show* went national, no one was talking about Phil Donahue as the king of TV talk anymore. Instead, Oprah and her show were considered tops in daytime talk television.

Winfrey now looked to her attorney and Harpo Production partner Jeffrey Jacobs to help her develop a way to include more film projects and acting opportunities in her career. For Winfrey to gain control of her own schedule, her production company, Harpo, needed to assume ownership and production responsibilities of *The Oprah Winfrey Show*. Her lawyer encouraged the idea, Winfrey explained. "He says, 'You can own your own show, and there is a studio that is the old Fred Niles studio that is going to become available. It needs a lot of work.'"

Jacobs began negotiating with both Capitol Cities/ABC and King World. Winfrey felt so strongly about the issue that during negotiations, she threatened to drop the show after her contract expired in 1991. Finally, in October 1988, Harpo Productions, Inc., gained ownership and production responsibilities of *The Oprah Winfrey Show*. Winfrey was free to produce her show without having to answer to anyone else about its content or when she would need to take time off to work on a film or go on remote locations for a particular show theme or audience. She was the first woman in history to own and produce her own talk show.

Following Jacobs' suggestion, Winfrey ended up purchasing a cluster of buildings that included an old film studio. It had been used previously by a production company that shot films, TV commercials, and TV shows. The facility took up one square block in an area near downtown Chicago, not far from the WLS-TV studios where *The Oprah Winfrey Show* had been taped for the past four years. Winfrey explained, "[T]he studio came about as a result of me wanting more time and creativity and control for myself. I bought the studio so that I would be able to act and do the show at the same time. So that I would be able to do two things that were very important to me."

Winfrey bought the property for $10 million. She then invested an additional $10 million to renovate and remodel the studio, creating a state-of-the-art television and film

The Harpo Studios building where *The Oprah Winfrey Show* is filmed. *(Courtesy of Kim Karpeles/Alamy)*

production facility. Harpo Studios is a 100,000-square-foot production studio with three sound stages, and it also offers screening rooms, kitchen facilities, offices, and a gym. The only show regularly produced there is *The Oprah Winfrey Show.*

Although Winfrey now owned her show and had complete control of its content, CAP Cities/ABC and King World were still an integral part of the continued life of *The Oprah Winfrey Show.* The television network guaranteed those stations owned and operated by ABC would continue to air the show for the next five years. King World worked out an agreement to continue to distribute the show until 1993.

Before the founding of Harpo, Inc., only two women—silent film star Mary Pickford, and television comedy star Lucille Ball—had established their own production companies in the entertainment industry. Not only was Winfrey the first woman to do so in more than thirty years, she was also the first African American woman to launch such a remarkable venture.

Mary Pickford *(Library of Congress)*

Harpo Productions' first creative project was a television miniseries adapted from *The Women of Brewster Place*, a 1982 novel by Gloria Naylor. Winfrey starred and served as executive producer of the program, which was a joint venture between Harpo and ABC.

The Women of Brewster Place involves seven black women living in a dilapidated tenement in an inner-city neighborhood. Each of the characters, who are dealing with various personal struggles, brings a unique personality to the Brewster Place sisterhood. *People* magazine writer Joanne Kaufman described the *The Women of Brewster Place* as "a story of broken dreams, betrayal, bitterness and survival."

Winfrey identified with the story, saying anyone who has lived as a black person in America could relate to the Brewster women, for they were one's mother, or aunt, or sister, or cousin. She explained that the story was about "maintaining your dignity in a world that tries to strip you of it." As Mattie Michael, Winfrey took on the role of the matriarch of the group, providing comfort and strength to the others as they deal with their individual issues.

Broadcast in 1989, the miniseries attracted some of the most renowned black actors in the industry, including Emmy Award winners Cecily Tyson, Jackée Harry, Lynn Whitfield, Olivia Cole, and Paul Winfield. Although the program received mixed reviews, executives at ABC decided to create a television series based on the miniseries. Called *Brewster Place,* the weekly series was broadcast in May 1990, but cancelled after only four episodes. However, executives with ABC were so impressed by the venture with Oprah and Harpo Productions that an agreement was worked out for the production of another four movies, with Winfrey starring in two of them.

Winfrey continued to receive honors and recognition for her work in film and television. At the end of 1988, she had been presented with the International Radio and Television Society's Broadcaster of the Year Award. At that time she was the youngest person ever chosen to receive the award— and just the fifth woman. In 1989, she received the NAACP (National Association for the Advancement of Colored People) Entertainer of the Year Award. In the years that followed, Winfrey would be honored with several NAACP Image Awards, which were established to recognize African Americans each year in the entertainment community.

The 1980s were also significant for Winfrey in that she established what would become a long-term relationship. She had dated several men during her twenties and early thirties; she would later say some were poor choices. But in April 1986, she found happiness with Stedman Graham. The tall businessman had recently founded the nonprofit organization Athletes Against Drugs—an organization that teaches kids about the dangers of drugs.

Before the two began dating, Graham had met Winfrey on several occasions at social events around Chicago. She was initially wary of him, but soon found him to be charming, polite, and genuine. In 1986, Winfrey expressed her satis- faction with the relationship, telling *People* magazine, "He's kind, and he's supportive, and he's 6'6"!" In 1992, Stedman Graham and Oprah Winfrey announced their engagement, but although they have been together for more than twenty years, they have yet to marry. They live together in a condo- minium on Chicago's "Gold Coast"—so named because the area north of the downtown business district and along the lakefront is considered the city's wealthiest neighborhood.

Winfrey and Stedman Graham in 1987 *(Courtesy of Ron Galella/ WireImage)*

FIVE

Finding Herself, Helping Others

While busy with her show and getting Harpo Productions, Inc. off the ground, Winfrey realized that she had one unfinished piece of business in her life to address—earning her college degree. In order to launch her broadcasting career, she had left Tennessee State University (TSU) before graduating. But she had promised herself that one day she would return to finish her requirements and get her degree.

In 1987, after she won her first Emmy, Winfrey was asked to give the commencement speech at TSU. She agreed, but on the condition that she would be allowed to finish up her own class requirements and be able to graduate along with the class.

That May, at the TSU graduation ceremonies, Winfrey received her degree and delivered the commencement address. During her talk, she reiterated her passionate belief in the importance of a good education, stressing how important it is to one's future success in life. Winfrey also announced that in honor of her father, Vernon, she would endow ten financial need and academic merit scholarships, valued at more than $70,000 each, to be awarded to TSU students. Since 1987, Winfrey has contributed $250,000 to this scholarship fund each year.

Winfrey shared her growing wealth in other ways. As her success and that of her show continued to climb, she rewarded a few of her key staffers at the end of 1987 by taking them to New York City for a Christmas shopping spree. The group took a limo ride to Bergdorf Goodman's, a posh luxury department store on Fifth Avenue in midtown Manhattan, where they were given an "allowance" to spend however they pleased. The shopping spree continued the next day, when Winfrey took the group to buy shoes and then visited a New York furrier, where she paid for each staff member's choice of a fur coat.

Members of Winfrey's family also shared in her good fortune. Winfrey quietly provided financial support for her half sister, Patricia, and half brother, Jeffrey, as well as for Patricia's two daughters, Chrishaunda and Alicia. Patricia had a serious problem with substance abuse and was not able to care for the girls. Eventually, Winfrey helped Patricia enter a drug rehabilitation facility and sent her nieces to live with her mother Vernita. (Winfrey would later pay for the girls to attend school. Patricia would die in 2003 of drug-related causes.)

Jeffrey died in 1989, after contracting acquired immunodeficiency syndrome (AIDS), a disease that damages the body's immune system. After her half-brother's death, Winfrey released a statement, saying, "My family, like thousands of others throughout the world, grieves not just for the death of one young man, but for the many unfulfilled dreams and accomplishments that society has been denied because of AIDS."

The desire to help others financially reached beyond friends, family, and co-workers. After making the scholarship endowment to her alma mater, Winfrey saw that her wealth could allow her to help people she had never met. In 1987, she established The Oprah Winfrey Foundation, an organization "committed to empowering women, children, and families by furthering education and welfare for low-opportunity communities around the world." Through the foundation, she pointed out, "we have awarded hundreds of grants to organizations that carry out this vision. It provides teacher education and scholarships to students who are determined to use their education to give back to their communities in the U.S. and abroad. [It] contributes school supplies and builds schools to educate thousands of underserved children internationally."

As her media empire grew, Winfrey devoted more of her time and money to charitable endeavors. In a 1991 interview she talked about the importance of giving back: "I don't think you ever stop giving. I really don't. I think it's an on-going process. And it's not just about being able to write a check. It's being able to touch somebody's life."

Following her conviction that education is key to improving the world, Winfrey donates hundreds of thousands of dollars to schools in need and has established scholarship funds at various educational institutions throughout the country.

When Morehouse College, in Atlanta, Georgia, decided to present Winfrey with an honorary doctorate degree at its 1990 commencement, she returned the honor by donating $1 million to the school, for use as the Oprah Winfrey Endowment Scholarship Fund. As of 2004, Winfrey had donated $12 million to the school, a contribution that has enabled 250 students to continue or complete their education at the private, all-male historically black institution.

In 1995, Winfrey would again make a difference in the lives of students when she made a $1 million donation to Spelman College in Atlanta, Georgia, a college attended primarily by black female students. Winfrey designated the money to be used in environmental biology and chemistry research.

The ability to make these financial contributions is due to the enormous success of Winfrey's television talk show, which continued to be popular throughout the 1980s and 1990s. She presented topics on the show that she thought would interest her predominantly female audiences, as well as those subjects she believed to be timely or important.

One show, broadcast in May 1990, proved to be a turning point for Winfrey in her own life. Always outgoing and energetic during the tapings of her shows, Oprah often shared private issues such as her battle with her weight or her relationship with boyfriend Stedman Graham. She had even given glimpses into the difficulties of her past—of being an illegitimate child, having been raised by her grandmother, and growing up poor and black in the South. But Winfrey was very private about certain aspects of her life. She did not talk openly about the sexual abuse that had shaped her life as a teenager and young woman.

During the taping of her May 21 show, however, Winfrey opened the door to her past while interviewing Truddi Chase, author of *When Rabbits Howl*. The book tells the story of how Truddi, who had been sexually abused by her stepfather from the age of two until she was sixteen, had developed multiple personalities to deal with the trauma.

As Winfrey interviewed Chase, her own memories of the trauma of being sexually abused became overwhelming. When Chase explained how the abuse caused her to believe she was a bad person and that she was to blame for her misery, Winfrey identified with the words. "I think it was on that day that, for the first time, I recognized that I was not to blame," Winfrey explained later:

> I became a sexually promiscuous teenager and as a result of that got myself into a lot of trouble, and believed that I was responsible for it. It wasn't until I was thirty-six years old, thirty-six, that I connected the fact, 'Oh that's why I was that way.' . . . I still believed I was responsible somehow. That I was a bad girl.

As she came to that realization in front of her studio audience and millions of viewers around the country, Winfrey finally understood that she was not to blame for what had happened to her. She lost control of her emotions and began crying uncontrollably. "I thought I was going to have a breakdown on television," she later admitted. "And I said, 'Stop! Stop! You've got to stop rolling cameras!' And they didn't, so I got myself through it, but it was really quite traumatic for me."

Once her story was out in the open, Winfrey decided to encourage other victims of abuse to stop suppressing their feelings and to speak out. "A part of my mission in life now is to encourage every other child who has been abused to tell," says Winfrey. "You tell, and if they don't believe you,

you keep telling. You tell everybody until someone listens to you."

The following November, determined to do more than just talk about the need for change, Winfrey went to Washington, D.C., where she testified before members of the U.S. Senate Judiciary Committee to lobby for passage of the National Childhood Protection Act. The legislation called for the establishment of a searchable national database of convicted offenders for use by employers working with children. A search on the database would keep anyone with a history of abusing children from being hired for jobs that put them in contact with kids. Three years later, on December 20, 1993, as an invited guest at the White House, Winfrey stood beside

Winfrey stands behind President Clinton as he signs the National Childhood Protection Act. *(Courtesy of Cynthia Johnson/Getty Images)*

President Bill Clinton as he signed the National Childhood Protection Act into law. For her efforts in getting the law passed, the law was nicknamed the Oprah Bill.

Winfrey continued to use her entertainment business to keep the subject of child abuse, as well as other issues, in the public mind. She worked out a deal with ABC to produce after-school specials that dealt with other concerns affecting children and teens. Among the made-for-television movies was *Scared Silent: Exposing and Ending Child Abuse,* which aired on Friday, September 4, 1992. In an unprecedented move, the Public Broadcasting Service (PBS) along with both CBS and the National Broadcasting Company (NBC) networks carried the broadcast simultaneously. The response was significant. During and following the broadcast, more than 112,000 calls came through the Childhelp/IOF Foresters National Child Abuse Hotline.

Another message that Winfrey presented to the public was the devastating effect of poverty and violent neighborhoods on children. In 1993, Harpo produced *There Are No Children Here*, a TV movie based on Alex Kotlowitz's 1991 book about children in Henry Horner Homes, a low-income housing project in Chicago. The title comes from a comment made by the mother of two boys who lived in the violent neighborhood: "[T]here are no children here. They've seen too much to be children."

Using the $500,000 earned from making the movie, Winfrey set up the charity Families for a Better Life. The money is used to help families living in poverty around the country obtain jobs, life counseling, and acquire new homes in safer neighborhoods.

Winfrey received an Emmy for "Shades of a Single Protein," which appeared on the *ABC Afterschool Specials* series in January 1993. During the program, in which Winfrey discussed race relations with teens, she explained the rationale behind the title, saying "Black people are not black and white people are not white. We're all really different shades of a single protein that we call melanin."

Some issues taken on by the popular talk show host were not as serious. A regular concern that Oprah brought up on *The Oprah Winfrey Show* was her problems with dieting and weight loss. During one memorable show in November 1986, she wheeled sixty-seven pounds of animal fat onstage to illustrate the amount of weight she lost while on a liquid diet. However, she soon gained back the weight, and dieting remained an ongoing battle, as she freely shared her setbacks and failures with her audience. In 1991, Winfrey told *People* magazine, "My greatest failure was in believing that the weight issue was just about the weight. It's about not handling stress properly." As a result, she turned to daily exercise and weight training, as well as a diet with no refined sugars or starches.

Winfrey decided to pass along some food tips by developing a cookbook in conjunction with her personal chef Rosie Daley. All the recipes were low-fat, healthy meal alternatives to the high fat, higher calorie foods she used to eat. *In the Kitchen with Rosie: Oprah's Favorite Recipes,* published in 1994, became a best seller after Winfrey promoted the book on her show.

Continuing her venture in self-help publishing, Winfrey put out a second book two years later with her personal trainer Bob Greene. *Make the Connection: Ten Steps to a Better*

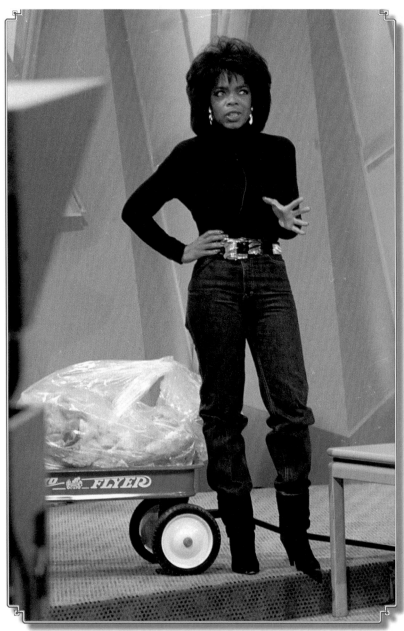

Winfrey appears on her show with sixty-seven pounds of animal fat to illustrate the amount of weight she lost while on a liquid diet in 1986. *(Courtesy of AP Images/Charles Bennet)*

Rosie Daley *(Courtesy of Tom Maday/Time Life Pictures/Getty Images)*

Body and a Better Life, published in 1996, focused on the importance of diet and exercise. Winfrey said she published the book to share her tips with people who are struggling with the same problems as she had.

The nineties had seen Winfrey getting serious about being fit and healthy, and she even trained as a long-distance runner.

In August 1993, Winfrey participated in the America's Finest City Half-Marathon (10-K race) in San Diego, California, finishing in a respectable 2:16:00. She was so energized by her success that she told Greene she wanted to train to run a full marathon—the 26.2-mile Marine Corps Marathon in Washington, D.C. On October 23, 1994, Winfrey ran alongside Greene, completing the race in a respectable four and a half hours.

SIX

Positive Image

In 1994, Winfrey signed a contract with King World in which she agreed to continue producing *The Oprah Winfrey Show* though 2000. At that time she obtained more than a million shares of King World Productions, becoming one of that company's largest shareholders. By 1996 her estimated personal worth was $98 million.

In May of 1996, Winfrey received one of the most prestigious awards in broadcasting. She was presented with the George Foster Peabody Award presented for distinguished achievement and exemplary public service in the media. Around the same time she also received the International Radio and Television Society's Gold Medal, awarded to acknowledge significant career-long contributions to the electronic media industry.

By that point, however, Winfrey had made serious changes to her show. Throughout the 1980s, new talk shows had

Winfrey holding her Peabody Award. *(Courtesy of Jerzy Dabrowski/ZUMA Press)*

cropped up on the daytime television circuit to compete with Donahue and Winfrey's programs. By the early 1990s, talk show programs in general had undergone a change, opting for an edgier and more provocative tone.

Hosted by personalities like Geraldo Rivera, Sally Jesse Raphael, Jerry Springer, and Jenny Jones, the new shows presented topics intended to draw viewers through their shock value. For example, Jerry Springer hosted shows in which married couples revealed their infidelities to each other, or feuding families became so violent that they had to be separated by Springer's production staff.

As early as 1988, *Washington Post* TV critic Tom Shales had lamented the decline of decent social and/or political show content on the talk show circuit. At that time he was the first to raise the issue of what the talk shows had become—trash TV. Winfrey was not immune from such criticisms, having aired shows with racy topics such as cross dressing, threesome relationships, and man hunting.

But in 1994, the talk show host decided that *The Oprah Winfrey Show* needed to move away from such topics and focus on ideas that would be uplifting and beneficial. Winfrey wanted her program to encourage people in their lives, not just cheaply entertain. In a 1995 interview with *TV Guide*, she explained, "I am embarrassed by how far over the line [talk show] topics have gone, but I also recognize my own contribution to this. People should not be surprised and humiliated on national television for the purpose of entertainment."

As part of fulfilling the promise to bring aspects to her show that affected audiences in a more positive manner, Winfrey introduced "Oprah's Book Club," in September 1996. As an on-air reading group, the book club initially featured

Winfrey holds one of her "Oprah's Book Club" books on her show in 2007. *(Courtesy of AP Images/Harpo Productions, George Burns)*

contemporary books, beginning with Jacquelyn Mitchard's *The Deep End of the Ocean.* Each month Winfrey selected a book for her audience to read, and then had the author of that book on her show the next month.

Since the show's viewing audience typically ranged from 15 to 20 million, any Oprah selection became an instant best seller. Publishers soon saw the result of Oprah's influence. A book selected for the Oprah Book Club averaged sales of more than a million copies. Some publishers estimate that Oprah's power to sell a book is from twenty to one hundred times greater than that of any other celebrity. In 1997 *Newsweek* named Oprah Winfrey the "Most Important Person in Books and Media," no doubt for her Book Club involvement.

Giving positive messages was part of Winfrey's commencement speech that she gave in May 1997, when Stedman Graham's daughter graduated from Wellesley College, in Wellesley, Massachusetts. Winfrey shared five important lessons that she said had made her life better:

> 1. Life is a journey. Everyday experiences will teach you who you really are.
>
> 2. When people show you who they are, believe them the first time. This is especially helpful with men. Don't force them to beat you over the head with the message.
>
> 3. Turn your wounds into wisdom. Everyone makes mistakes. They are just God's way of telling you you're moving in the wrong direction.
>
> 4. Be grateful. Keep a daily journal of the things you are thankful for. It will keep you focused on the abundance in your life.
>
> 5. Create the highest, grandest vision possible for your life, because you become what you believe.

The Oprah Winfrey Show remains the core business and economic force from which Winfrey's many other projects evolved. The revenue from syndication of the talk show has supported many of Winfrey's philanthropic activities. In addition, the television show also provides a venue to a wide audience.

On her show of September 18, 1997, Winfrey made an announcement that would heighten the public's affection for her and underscore the positive influence she wanted to make on the world. Having long wanted to increase her charitable involvement and contributions to worthwhile causes, Winfrey decided to use her show to get people involved more in giving back, as well as motivate them to actively participate in charitable projects.

To accomplish this goal, Winfrey announced the creation of "The World's Largest Piggy Bank." As part of the September show, she invited viewers to contribute their spare change to the piggy bank. The funds raised, she explained, would be used to create scholarships to send disadvantaged kids to college and for other charitable organizations.

The piggy bank campaign raised more than $1 million. Winfrey matched that amount, and other donors gave funds. Ultimately, Oprah's Angel Network—as the campaign came to be called—collected more than $3 million.

Funds from Oprah's Angel Network are distributed in the form of grants and scholarships. The money has been used to help rebuild communities devastated by hurricanes Katrina and Rita in Texas, Mississippi, Louisiana, and Alabama. Angel Network funds have also been used to construct more than fifty schools in twelve impoverished countries, and provide more than $1 million worth of school supplies, uniforms, and shoes to 18,000 poverty-stricken children in South Africa. Some of the organizations that have been recipients of funds from the Angel Network include Habitat for Humanity, Hurricane Katrina and Rita: Relief & Recovery, B.I.K.E., and the Children's Health Fund.

Oprah Winfrey's goal of sharing positive messages with the public has also been accomplished through her movie company, Harpo Films. Established in 1990 as a division of Harpo Productions, Inc., the company is based in Los Angeles, California. Harpo Films brings stories that Winfrey believes have important messages to television and movie screens. In the 1980s, she had purchased the rights to several classic and contemporary novels. They included Toni Morrison's 1987 novel *Beloved* and Zora Neal Hurston's *Their Eyes Were Watching God*, published in 1937.

In bringing Toni Morrison's Pulitzer prize-winning novel *Beloved* to the big screen, Winfrey served as producer and

Winfrey and actress Kimberly Elise in a scene from the movie *Beloved*. *(Courtesy of Touchstone Pictures/ZUMA Press)*

took on the role of Sethe, an escaped plantation slave who is haunted by the ghost of her daughter, Beloved. Sethe had killed the girl rather than have her returned to slavery. The story, which takes place in Ohio during the 1870s, reveals the brutality of slavery while also presenting the tale of Beloved haunting her mother.

Directed by Academy Award-winner Jonathan Demme, and also starring Danny Glover, *Beloved* was released in mid-October 1998. For Winfrey, making the film was the fulfillment of a lifelong dream, but the movie did not resonate well with the viewing audience. *Beloved* earned just $23 million, less than half of what it had cost to make. A year after the movie's release, Winfrey explained how she felt about the box-office failure: "I just expected, oh, it's going to be great in the box office, and so it was such a disappointment. . . . this was the only time that my expectations really let me down."

Under the banner "Oprah Winfrey Presents," Harpo Films creates telefilms as part of a long-term agreement made with the ABC Television Network and Disney in 1995. The first Oprah Winfrey Presents made-for-television movie was *Before Women Had Wings* (1997). Based on the novel by Connie May Fowler, the story centers on nine-year-old Avocet Abigail Jackson, whose life in poverty and abuse does not diminish her love for her parents. Winfrey plays Miss Zora, a black woman and neighbor who teaches Jackson about dignity in the face of adversity. The movie received numerous award nominations, and it won an Emmy for Ellen Barkin (Outstanding Lead Actress in a Miniseries or a Movie), who portrayed Jackson's mother in the movie. The film also ranked as one of the top ten made-for-television movies of the year.

One of the Oprah Winfrey Presents films was *The Wedding* (1998), based on Dorothy West's novel about a well-off black family living on Martha's Vineyard. The two-part miniseries, which dealt with race and class, starred Halle Berry. The actress would later appear in another Oprah Winfrey production, *Their Eyes Were Watching God* (2005), an adaptation of the novel by Zora Neale Hurston. Other novel adaptations that Harpo Films brought to the television screen include Theodore Rubin's *David and Lisa* (1998), Mitch Albom's *Tuesdays With Morrie* (1999), and Elizabeth Strout's *Amy and Isabelle* (2001).

Many Harpo Films television projects have received Emmy and Golden Globe nominations and awards for superior acting and production. Quality is important to Winfrey, who holds the film company to high standards. Harpo typically produces only about one movie per year because she also has specific rules about what stories can become films. For example, one policy is that she will not make a movie based on a book that she has endorsed.

Like her standards for films carrying the Harpo name, Winfrey's standards for *The Oprah Winfrey Show* reflect a desire to inform, teach, and help the public. In 1998, Winfrey officially named the focus of her television talk show "Change Your Life TV." She believes that even the most tragic event can result in something positive:

> [M]y intention is always, regardless of what the show is—whether it's about sibling rivalry or wife battering or children of divorce—for people to see within each show that you are responsible for your life, that although there may be tragedy in your life, there's always a possibility to triumph. It doesn't

matter who you are, where you come from. The ability to triumph begins with you. Always, always.

Throughout the 1990s, Winfrey had reigned supreme as *The Oprah Winfrey Show* retained its position year after year as the number-one rated talk show. In 1998, she received her seventh Emmy for Outstanding Talk Show Host, and the ninth Emmy for *The Oprah Winfrey Show*. That year, she was also awarded the Lifetime Achievement Award from the National Academy of Television Arts and Sciences. Subsequently, Winfrey removed herself from future Emmy consideration. Overall, she and her television program had won a total of forty Daytime Emmys (more than twenty had also been awarded in the Creative Arts categories).

That same year, *Time* magazine recognized Winfrey and her show by naming her one of its one hundred most influential people of the twentieth century. The magazine noted that at age forty-four, Winfrey had a net worth of more than half a billion dollars.

The influence of Winfrey and her talk show remained strong during the 1990s. The books that she chose for her book club become instant best sellers. Any negative comments she would make about a particular product could have a negative impact on sales.

For example, in 1995, *The Oprah Winfrey Show* did a story on mad cow disease. This deadly and debilitating illness in humans causes the slow destruction of brain tissue. During the course of the episode, Winfrey stated her concerns about the possibility of contracting the disease by eating. She made a statement that this knowledge "just stopped me cold from eating another burger."

OCTOBER 5, 1998 $2.95

www.time.com

STARR: TRIPPED UP?
HEROES FOR THE PLANET

The most
successful
woman on
TV fulfills
a dream
by returning
to movies
in a story
about slavery,
passion and
family. An
exclusive
visit with...

The
Beloved
Oprah

Winfrey on the cover of Time magazine in 1998. *(Courtesy of Ken Regan/
Time Magazine/Time & Life Pictures/Getty Images)*

Disturbed about the effect her words could have on the beef industry, Texas cattlemen brought a multimillion-dollar lawsuit for libel against Winfrey in 1996 (a 1995 Texas law states that people can be held liable if they make negative statements about certain foods). The cattlemen claimed that Winfrey's comments during the show had resulted in a downturn in the U.S. beef market. She fought the defamation charges in a court trial held in early 1998 in Amarilla, Texas. During the six-week trial, she taped her show in Amarilla. Ultimately, the jury came out in favor of Winfrey's First Amendment rights and she won the case.

During the course of the trial in Texas, Winfrey hired a psychologist named Phil McGraw to assist with her case. In the years that followed, he became a regular guest on *The Oprah Winfrey Show*, giving advice on dealing with life relationships. Bringing McGraw on the show as a regular contributor would soon lead to more additions to the O Empire.

SEVEN

Adding to the O Empire

Toward the end of the 1990s and in the beginning of the 2000s, Oprah Winfrey invested in new companies and developed new Harpo projects, while continuing to keep her talk show in the number one position. When it was time to extend her contract with King World Productions, in 1998, the syndication company was depending on *The Oprah Winfrey Show* for approximately 40 percent of its annual revenue. As a result, King World agreed to pay Harpo Productions $150 million to renew the contract through the 2001-2002 television seasons. The show, syndicated worldwide, claimed a viewership at the time of approximately 20 million people.

In 1999, Winfrey's Web site, Oprah.com, launched the previous year in a joint effort between ABC Internet Group and Harpo Productions, was redesigned. The site contained advice, interactive workbooks, photos, videos, inspirational stories, books, and other features, including information on

The Oprah Winfrey Show, and various public charity efforts supported by Winfrey. Today, Oprah.com averages more than 70-million page views per month, and claims more than 6 million users. According to the Web site, it receives about 20,000 e-mails per week and more than 6 million people visit Oprah.com monthly.

In addition to establishing a presence in the Internet, Winfrey entered into the cable channel industry. In December 1998, she announced that she was forming a partnership with Geraldine Laybourne (the former president of Nickelodeon) and television producers Marcy Carsey, Tom Werner, and Caryn Mandelbach. They founded Oxygen Media, LLC, a women's cable television network and Web service. Based in New York City, the diversified media company was also backed by America Online and ABC. As part of Winfrey's investment in Oxygen Media, she contributed $20 million and certain rights to past episodes of *The Oprah Winfrey Show*. In return, she held a 25 percent stake in the network.

Winfrey's initial contribution to the cable television channel, which launched in March 2000, was to host a twelve-part series on how to navigate around the Internet. Winfrey later produced and hosted a show for the channel called *Use Your Life*, a half-hour series recognizing people who had helped bring about positive change in the lives of others. In 2002, the talk show host introduced *Oprah After the Show* on the Oxygen network. Consisting of an unscripted, spontaneous thirty-minutes of talk, the show occurs after the taping of her daily syndicated show.

However, Winfrey's biggest venture in 2000 was helping to launch a new women's lifestyle magazine as part of a joint venture with Hearst Magazines and her own company, called Harpo Print, LLC. Hearst had guaranteed Winfrey total editorial control over the new magazine, which was called *O, The Oprah Magazine.* (Since most of Winfrey's friends refer to her as O, the name seemed perfect for the new publication).

Winfrey enlisted the help of best friend and television anchorwoman Gayle King, who was named editor-at-large of *O.* In this capacity, she was to work with editor-in-chief Ellen Kunes to ensure that the magazine reflected what Winfrey, as editorial director, wanted in what she described as a "personal-growth manual."

The first issue of *O*, published in April 2000, sold out its 1.5 million issues on the newsstands. However, disagreement over the direction of the writing and design soon led to the resignation of Kunes, who was replaced in July 2001 by a new editor in chief, Amy Gross, who has remained in the position ever since. In a January 2001 story in *Newsweek*, Winfrey addressed criticisms that she was too controlling and involved in all the details of the magazine: "I wasn't too controlling. I needed to be involved. When you get me, you are not getting an image. You are not getting a figurehead. You're not getting a theme song. You're getting all of me."

O, The Oprah Magazine features Winfrey on every cover and contains her monthly column, called "What I Know for Sure." She has admitted that she is very concerned that the magazine contents are just right. In a 2002 interview with *Fortune* magazine, Winfrey explained that she reads every word and approves every picture before *O* is sent to the printer. *O* editor Gayle King agreed, saying at the time, "She's into every little niggly thing—the commas, the exclamation

Winfrey speaks at a press conference held to announce the launch of
O, The Oprah Magazine. (Courtesy of AP Images/Ed Bailey)

points." It was reported that Winfrey spent five to six hours a day working on the publication.

Magazine publishing can be a risky enterprise. Only 10 to 20 percent of new magazines ever become successful, and it generally takes three to five years before a new publication shows a profit. However, *O, The Oprah Magazine* was successful from the start. It has been credited with being the most triumphant magazine launch in the past several years: it was initially published every two months, but quickly evolved into a monthly publication. After just seven issues, *O* had a circulation of 2 million.

In an effort to continue to reach a broader audience, Winfrey took *O* to an international audience, launching her first edition in South Africa in April 2002. In 2007, the magazine was selling an average of 2.4 million copies a month.

Winfrey continued to expand her media empire, with the launch of a new daily show, the first new syndicated program produced by Harpo Productions. September 2002 saw the premiere of *The Dr. Phil Show,* hosted by family psychologist Philip McGraw. McGraw had been a frequent guest and resident expert on *The Oprah Winfrey Show.* McGraw was grateful to Winfrey for the opportunity to have his own show, explaining, "It was [Winfrey's] vision about me and what I could do that put me in the direction I've taken with my life. She's just a great resource, a great mentor . . . and I'm lucky to say, a very good and dear friend."

The Oprah Winfrey Show features several other experts, who provide advice and suggestions for self-improvement. Winfrey's longtime personal trainer and exercise physiologist Bob Greene appears regularly on the program. Heart surgeon Dr. Mehmet Oz offers health advice, while Jean

Chatzky provides information related to financial matters. Design expert Nate Berkus gives tips on home décor, while Dr. Robin Smith, a licensed psychologist and author, serves as "therapist-in-residence" on the show.

Many of these *Oprah Winfrey Show* experts also contribute to other Harpo efforts. McGraw and Greene are regular contributors to *O, The Oprah Magazine* (McGraw writes a monthly column). Interior designer Nate Berkus

Dr. Phil McGraw *(Courtesy of AP Images)*

is a regular contributor to *O at Home* magazine, a quarterly shelter magazine that launched in 2004.

In the fall of 2006, King World Productions, Scripps Networks, and Harpo Productions, Inc., combined forces to create a new talk show. The daily, one-hour program, hosted by Food Network personality and cookbook author Rachael Ray, began airing in September 2006.

In addition to increasing her business efforts, Winfrey looked to expand her philanthropic efforts. She had been inspired in 2000, when she and Stedman Graham traveled to South Africa where they were guests at the home of Nelson Mandela, the former president of South Africa. During this trip to South Africa, Winfrey saw many families living in extreme poverty, in homes with no indoor plumbing, and getting by with only the barest necessities. AIDS had devastated some regions: one in eight South Africans is HIV-positive.

Two years later after her initial visit, Winfrey returned to South Africa, where she launched an initiative she called "ChristmasKindness 2002". Over the course of twenty-one days, Winfrey, her staff, and friends hand-delivered gifts to people in two of the main provinces hardest hit by the AIDS epidemic—KwaZulu Natal and the Eastern Cape. They visited orphanages and schools, bringing thousands of children clothing, school supplies, shoes, toys, and sporting equipment.

Upon her return to the United States, Winfrey explained on her Web site the impact that ChristmasKindness had on her:

> My life was dramatically changed last Christmas when I went
> to South Africa on a mission to bring Christmas joy to 50,000

Rachael Ray *(Courtesy of AP Images)*

children. I realized in those moments why I was born, why I am not married and do not have children of my own. *These* are my children. I made a decision to be a voice for those children, to empower them, to help educate them, so the spirit that burns alive inside each of them does not die.

Winfrey's commitment to South African children included a plan to build schools in the country. Before beginning the ChristmasKindness tour, Winfrey had thrust a shovel into the soil during a ceremony held on December 6, 2002, near Johannesburg. The planned project was the Oprah Winfrey Leadership Academy for Girls, a state-of–the-art boarding school for seventh- through twelfth-grade students.

Winfrey explained her purpose for creating the Leadership Academy for Girls, which cost approximately $40 million and took about five years of planning: "What I wanted to do is give an opportunity to girls who were like me—girls who were poor, who had come from disadvantaged circumstances, but girls who had a light so bright that not even poverty, disease, and life circumstances could dim that light. . . . This school is a symbol of leadership for all of Africa."

The Leadership Academy for Girls officially opened on January 2, 2007, in the town of Henly-on-Klip, about forty miles outside Johannesburg. Winfrey was there at the ribbon-cutting ceremony, along with some of the 152 girls making up the first class. The school will eventually serve 450, making it possible to educate close to 5,000 girls in a ten-year period. The first 152 were chosen from all nine South African provinces.

More than 3,500 girls showing exceptional leadership potential applied for 152 spots—Winfrey interviewed the five-hundred finalists. "It's my vision that this academy will help to develop the future leaders of South Africa and be a source of pride for South Africans for generations to come," she explains. The ceremony marked the end of the five-year project and the beginning of a new life for the girls who would be attending. Also in attendance at the school's opening ceremony were former South African president Nelson Mandela, movie director Spike Lee, and entertainers Mariah Carey and Tina Turner.

The new school's twenty-eight buildings and fifty-acre campus are lavishly designed. The institution includes state-of-the-art classrooms, computer and science labs, a library, theater, gym, fields for a variety of sports, a dining hall, and dormitories that rival some hotel accommodations. Winfrey explained that the school's design was important to her:

> From the very beginning of designing this school, I wanted this to be an environment where the girls could be consistently inspired. I wanted these girls to have the best—the best campus, the best curriculum and, of course, the best opportunities. It's not just about academic learning; it's about social, emotional, and spiritual learning. This school represents a symbol for what is possible for African girls. I believe that if you're surrounded by beautiful things, if you're surrounded by wonderful teachers who are there to inspire you, if you're surrounded by beauty, it brings out the beauty in you.

Winfrey opened a second school in South Africa on March 16, 2007. The Seven Fountains Primary School located in Kokstad, was funded by the Angel Network, and will serve as a primary school for more than one thousand students. The decision to build the schools in Africa, Winfrey explains, came about because of her desire to be more directly involved with her charitable works. "When I first started making a

Winfrey and Nelson Mandela break ground for the Oprah Winfrey
Leadership Academy for Girls in 2002. *(Courtesy of AP Images/Themba Hadebe)*

lot of money," she says, "I really became frustrated with the fact that all I did was write check after check to this or that charity without really feeling like it was a part of me. At a certain point, you want to feel that connection."

In 2004, Winfrey treated herself to a grandiose fiftieth birthday party with a four-day bash, complete with a special *Oprah Winfrey Show* "surprise party." Among the many guests who came in person or attended by satellite broadcast to extend their birthday wishes were Quincy Jones, Nelson Mandela, singer Tina Turner, Nobel Peace Prize-winner Desmond Tutu, and actor Tom Cruise. Winfrey blew out the candles on a four-hundred-pound birthday cake at the glamorous, black-tie party.

While Winfrey made the most out of treating herself for her fiftieth birthday, she particularly enjoys giving expensive gifts and treats to others. Some *Oprah Winfrey Show* episodes have been based on giving gifts to the members of her audience. "Oprah's Favorite Things" is an annual episode, first launched in 2002, that is typically taped around Thanksgiving (although the show's producers do not announce the actual date in advance). All information about the show is kept secret. During the course of the year, Winfrey publishes in *O* a list of favorite things that she has come across, whether it's a watch, a skin softening lotion, a bathrobe, or a jogging suit. At the "Oprah's Favorite Things" show, Winfrey gives everyone in the audience a selection from her list. Since the audience at Winfrey's talk show typically averages around three hundred people, millions of dollars of gifts may be given away.

Another popular feature on *The Oprah Winfrey Show* is the "Wildest Dreams" segment, which is based on the idea of making one's wildest dreams come true. One of the most well-known "Wildest Dreams" episodes occurred when the idea was first introduced in the fall of 2004. During the premiere of the nineteenth season of *The Oprah Winfrey Show*, Winfrey decided to surprise her audience with keys to a new Pontiac G-6 car, each with an estimated value of $28,000. (In this case, she had persuaded Pontiac to donate the cars.) On another "Wildest Dreams" show, Winfrey gave a four-year scholarship and $10,000 in clothing to a woman who had spent most of her life living either in foster homes or homeless shelters. The "Oprah's Wildest Dreams Come True" tour bus, complete with production staff and camera crews, travels around the country, answering the requests of a select few to have their wishes granted. The filming of their stories then becomes future episodes on the show.

EIGHT

The Oprah Legacy

With solid success in television, movies, magazine and book publishing, theater, and radio, Oprah Winfrey is an all-media magnate, and one of the most powerful women in the entertainment, publishing, and broadcast industries. In the May 2003 edition of *Forbes* magazine, which announced its annual list of America's billionaires, the publication noted that Winfrey was the first African American woman to join the club.

After naming Winfrey as one of the most influential people of the twentieth century, *Time* magazine has placed Winfrey on its annual list of the 100 Most Influential People in World. Since 1998, *Fortune* magazine has listed her on its list of the fifty most powerful women in business. In its November 2005 issue, the magazine placed her in its "Hall of Fame," for being among the top eight of the fifty most powerful women in business (those who chair a company or hold the position of chief executive officer).

Winfrey has long served as chairperson and CEO of the Harpo Productions, Inc. The company boasts about 350 employees. Its president and chief operating officer is Jeffrey D. Jacobs, while Douglas J. Pattison serves as chief financial officer. Another longtime executive is chief operations officer Tim Bennett, who was the program director for WLS-TV in Chicago when Winfrey first worked there.

In addition to her many business successes, Winfrey has continued to receive awards and honors for her role in the media and entertainment industries. In 2003, VH1 named her the greatest pop culture icon of all time (topping Superman and Elvis Presley). That same year, she received the Association of American Publishers' AAP Honors Award for significant achievement in promoting American books and authors. In 2004, Winfrey was named the People's Choice Awards' Favorite Talk Show Host, and she also received the United Nations Association of the United States of America's Global Humanitarian Action Award. In 2005, she was inducted into the NAACP Hall of Fame and received the National Civil Rights Museum 2005 National Freedom Award.

As the recipient of many awards, Winfrey wanted to bestow some honors on other African American women, particularly those who had come before her and who she believed had helped make her own successes possible. Following a year of careful planning, Winfrey sponsored a weekend celebration in May 2005 to pay homage to twenty-five women for their contributions to the arts, entertainment, and civil rights.

Winfrey called the celebration the Legends Ball; the list of honored guests included novelists Maya Angelou and Toni Morrison, the poet Nikki Giovanni, entertainers Aretha Franklin and Diana Ross, and civil rights activists Coretta

Winfrey with her 2004 People's Choice Award.
(Courtesy of AP Images/Mark J. Terrill)

Scott King. The three-day event featured a private luncheon at Winfrey's forty-two-acre estate, in Montecito, California; a Saturday evening ball at a resort in nearby Santa Barbara; and a Sunday gospel brunch back at Winfrey's California home.

During the tribute weekend, Winfrey enthused, "These women, who have been meaningful to so many of us over the years, are legends who have been magnificent in their pioneering and advancing of African-American women. It is because of their steps that our journey has no boundaries."

A story about the Legends Ball appeared in the August 2005 issue of *O*. A year later, highlights from the historic celebration were broadcast by the ABC Television Network as a one-hour special. Winfrey's friend Gayle King reported after the event: "Oprah told me this has been one of the most extraordinary events of her life."

Later that year, Winfrey added the title of "theater producer" to her ever-growing list of multimedia accomplishments. Twelve years after making her motion picture film debut in *The Color Purple*, a story of triumph over adversity, Winfrey helped bring about the story's adaptation into a stage musical. She joined with Quincy Jones, Roy Furman, and others to produce the show, which debuted on Broadway on December 2, 2005. The show received rave reviews, along with eleven Tony Award nominations, including Best Musical and Best Actress.

By the time *The Color Purple* closed on Broadway in February 2008, it had played more than nine hundred times and been seen by more than 1 million people. According to media reports, the $11 million musical had recouped the producers' investments in less than a year. The play was scheduled to continue to tour nationally until 2009.

Winfrey arriving at the 2005 Legends Ball. *(Courtesy of AP Images/Michael A. Mariant)*

In 2006, the technology of satellite radio created a new opportunity for Harpo Productions, Inc. September 25, 2006, saw the launching of Oprah & Friends, a new radio channel on XM Satellite Radio. Winfrey had signed a $55 million, three-year contract with XM Satellite to establish the new radio channel, which is produced by Harpo Radio, Inc.

Oprah & Friends broadcasts twenty-four hours a day, seven days a week, from a studio at Harpo headquarters, in Chicago. Its programming includes segments by contributors to the *The Oprah Winfrey Show* and *O, The Oprah Magazine*, including Robin Smith, Mehmet Oz, and Bob Greene. Winfrey and Gayle King provide a weekly half-hour radio show thirty-nine weeks per year.

Another film was produced by Harpo Films in December 2007: *The Great Debaters,* a movie inspired by the story of Melvin Tolson, a professor at the small African American school of Wiley College, in East Texas. Directed by Denzel Washington, who also stars as Professor Tolson, the film depicts how the Wiley debate team competes against racism and the team of an all-white school, during the 1930s. The film was nominated for several awards, including eight NAACP Image Awards and a Golden Globe for Best Picture, Drama.

Of the various departments within Harpo Entertainment, *The Oprah Winfrey Show,* produced by Harpo Productions and syndicated by King World, continues to bring in the most revenue, about $300 million per year. In 2004, Winfrey signed a contract extending its run through the 2010–2011 seasons. *O, The Oprah Magazine* (published monthly) and *O at Home* (published quarterly), produced by Harpo Print, LLC, and Hearst Magazines, also continue to do well.

However, Winfrey's connection with Oxygen Media was dissolved in the fall of 2007. Dissatisfied with the direction the Oxygen channel was taking, Winfrey and other Oxygen Media partners sold their interest in the company in October 2007 to NBC Universal for $925 million. Winfrey had not been as involved in the network, she later explained. She had no editorial control and noted that Oxygen "did not reflect my voice."

In an effort to establish a cable channel in which she would have control, Winfrey announced on January 15, 2008, the establishment of the Oprah Winfrey Network (OWN). The joint venture would be equally owned and advertising revenue split evenly between Winfrey's Harpo Productions and the media company Discovery Communications.

The new venture, designed to "entertain, inform and inspire people to live their best lives," includes cable television and the Oprah.com Web site. According to press releases, OWN will feature mostly original, nonfiction programming that focuses on the self-help and personal growth topics for which Winfrey is known. OWN will not carry her daily talk show, because the rights for that contract run through May 2011. The new channel is to debut in 2009.

With the formation of OWN, Winfrey achieved the "vision of creating my own network." In the joint announcement explaining the establishment of OWN, she stated: "Fifteen years ago, I wrote in my journal that one day I would create a television network, as I always felt my show was just the beginning of what the future could hold." Winfrey will serve as chairman and creative leader of the new network.

In an interview given shortly after the announcement, Winfrey explained,

> The truth of the matter is one day the [*Oprah Winfrey Show*] has to end. . . . [OWN] is an evolution of what I've been able to do every day. I will now have the opportunity to do that twenty-four hours a day on a platform that goes on forever. This network isn't just about me, it's using the voice and the brand and the vision, but it really is about creating possibilities for any number of people . . . to extend the vision in a way that obviously I cannot twenty-four hours a day.

Winfrey has long recognized that her name is her most valuable commodity. "There's no stronger brand in media than the Oprah brand," Discovery Communications chief executive David Zaslav has said. "Over the years, there's no one that's better at spotting talent and developing talent and, as chairman of this multimedia company, that's a big strength that we're going to lean on."

Gayle King has said the same thing: "Everybody's thinking, 'I gotta get a piece of that Oprah brand.'" But for many years, Winfrey's goal has been to maintain control over that brand. As a result, she has not formed many partnerships. Despite the alliances Winfrey has made with King World, ABC, Hearst, and Oxygen Media, she has kept Harpo privately owned. Winfrey has said, "If I lost control of the business, I'd lose myself—or at least the ability to be myself. Owning myself is a way to be myself."

Control over her name and her company policies have led to disagreements at times with her employees. Over the years, some staff members have complained about draconian policies at Harpo, Inc., but being in control has been and continues to be important to Winfrey. To prevent employee complaints from becoming public, she has required that employees at all levels sign a lifelong confidentially agreement. She believes that this provides protection for herself, her company, and the Oprah brand. She explained in an interview, "You wouldn't say [the policy was] harsh if you were in the tabloids all the time." She is protecting herself because her good name is her business.

Harpo Productions has most recently moved into producing prime time, reality television shows for ABC as well as TV movies. Oprah Winfrey's *The Big Give* gives contestants cash and other resources and challenges them to come up with creative and innovative ways to enrich the lives of other people. Contestants have eight weeks to give away the money as they develop ways to enrich the lives of strangers. The winner of the contest is the one who manages to give away the most money. The first prime-time series to be created by Harpo Productions, Inc. (in conjunction with Profiles Television Productions, LLC), *The Big Give* aired on ABC in March 2008.

A second reality show, entitled *Your Money or Your Life,* is under development at Harpo. The program features families dealing with a crisis. In each weekly episode, a team moves in with the family in an effort to help turn around their lives.

The themes of both reality shows—of giving back and helping others—have always been important to Winfrey. It has been reported that since reaching adulthood, she has donated at least 10 percent of her annual income to charity. In 2005, *BusinessWeek* named her the greatest black philanthropist in American history. At that time it was estimated that she had given about $303 million for various philanthropic purposes.

The exterior of the
Broadway Theater
where *The Color Purple*
debuted in 2005.
(Courtesy of AP Images)

According to GuideStar.org and federal tax filings, Winfrey runs three different charities: Oprah Winfrey's Angel Network, The Oprah Winfrey Operating Foundation, and The Oprah Winfrey Foundation. In 2004-2005, records show that the Angel Network distributed more than $4 million to forty organizations, gave $2 million in disaster relief, and claimed $15 million in net assets. For the same time period, The Oprah Winfrey Operating Foundation, which was set up for the Leadership Academy in South Africa, showed $19 million in assets. However, the bulk of philanthropic wealth is with the Oprah Winfrey Foundation. In 2006, it showed $172 million in total assets, and distributed $8 million to various educational, arts, and health care groups.

As of 2007 the Angel Network has raised more than $51 million. Because Oprah takes care of administrative costs, all money donated to the Angel Nework goes to the charity programs that it funds.

Most of Winfrey's philanthropy has reflected her passionate belief in the importance of education and her recognition that her wealth could provide opportunities to those in need. It is her belief that triumph over adversity is possible when one is provided with a good education. "Education is freedom. It provides the tools to affect one's own destiny," she has said. She has particularly tried to prove this belief via her establishment of the Leadership Academy for Girls in South Africa.

However, Winfrey has been criticized for spending money in Africa instead of doing more to help black Americans by opening schools in cities in the United States. Winfrey counters, though, that she has already provided millions of dollars to help educate children living in poverty in the United

States. Through her Oprah Winfrey Scholars Program, for example, she provides needs-based scholarships to students who commit to giving back to their hometown communities in the United States and overseas. She has admitted to being discouraged by American students who do not seem to appreciate their access to a free education. "I became so frustrated with visiting inner-city schools that I just stopped going," Winfrey told *Newsweek* magazine in January 2007. "The sense that you need to learn just isn't there."

However, Winfrey has donated and continues to contribute to efforts to help students in the United States. In 2006, she donated funds for the building of a $5 million facility to house a new Boys and Girls Club in her hometown of Kosciusko, Mississippi. The club will serve approximately

Winfrey stands with students during a ceremony to officially open her Leadership Academy for Girls in South Africa. *(Courtesy of AP Images/ Denis Farrell)*

three hundred children ages five through eighteen. The center contains computer labs, a music room, arts center, library, and gymnasium.

In October of 2006 Winfrey was devastated to learn that one of the school matrons of the Leadership Academy in South Africa had sexually abused several students. All too aware of the pain caused by sexual abuse, Winfrey immediately assumed responsibility for what had happened. She flew to South Africa, where she arranged for counselors and other help for the girls. She issued a public apology to the girls and their families, and looked to move on. "I think that all crisis is there to teach you about your life," Winfrey said later. "You have to be far more careful in choosing people to stand in the gap for you. You have to stay on it." In November, South African police arrested the former school matron and charged her with physical and sexual abuse.

As one of the most respected and admired public figures today, Winfrey has typically not used her influence outside of her business endeavors. However in 2007, she decided to voice her opinion in U.S. politics, and for the first time, officially endorsed a presidential candidate. In early May, while appearing on *Larry King Live*, on CNN, she publicly endorsed Barack Obama, an Illinois senator running for the Democratic presidential nomination. At the time, she stated, "I think that what [Obama] stands for, what he has proven that he can stand for, what he has shown, was worth me going out on a limb for." The following September, she sponsored a fundraiser that collected more than $3 million for the Obama campaign. She also actively campaigned in several states for the Illinois senator.

Winfrey stands on stage with presidential candidate Barack Obama and his wife Michelle during a campaign rally in 2007. *(Courtesy of AP Images/Elise Amendola)*

Despite being a billionaire and a celebrity, Winfrey derives her greatest pleasure through giving to others. "Making other people happy is what brings me happiness," Winfrey has said. "I have a blessed life, and I have always shared my life's gifts with others. I believe that to whom much is given, much is expected. So, I will continue to use my voice and my life as a catalyst for change, inspiring and encouraging people to help make a difference in the lives of others."

timeline

1954   Orpah (Oprah) Gail Winfrey born January 29, in Kosciusko, Mississippi.

1960   Moves to Milwaukee, Wisconsin, to live with mother, Vernita Lee.

1967   Receives scholarship to Nicolet High School in Milwaukee suburb of Glendale.

1968   Moves to Nashville, Tennessee, to live with father, Vernon Winfrey, and his wife, Zelma; gives birth prematurely to boy who dies soon afterward; attends East Nashville High School.

1971   Hired by WVOL to read news; enrolls at Tennessee State University (TSU).

1973   Becomes youngest news anchor and the first African American female news anchor at Nashville's WLAC-TV.

1976   Hired as co-anchor at WJZ-TV in Baltimore, Maryland.

1978   Co-hosts WJZ-TV's local talk show *People Are Talking*.

1983	Moves to Chicago, Illinois, to host WLS-TV's *A.M. Chicago.*
1984	Hires Jeffrey Jacobs as agent and business manager.
1985	Co-stars as Sofia in film *The Color Purple*; *A.M. Chicago* renamed *The Oprah Winfrey Show.*
1986	Nominated for Golden Globe and Academy Awards for Best Supporting Actress; establishes Harpo Productions, Inc.; *The Oprah Winfrey Show* enters syndication.
1987	Wins first Emmy for Best Talk/Service Show Host and Best Show.
1988	Buys film studio; obtains ownership and production rights to talk show.
1990	Establishes Harpo Films.
1991	Initiates the National Child Protection Act; the Oprah Bill signed into law in 1993.
1994	Publishes *In The Kitchen With Rosie: Oprah's Favorite Recipes*, with co-author Rosie Daley.
1995	Establishes Oprah.com; signs deal with ABC to produce six made-for-television films under banner of *Oprah Winfrey Presents.*

1996	Introduces monthly book club on *The Oprah Winfrey Show.*
1997	Establishes Oprah's Angel Network; wins a six-week libel trial in Amarillo, Texas.
1998	Becomes a partner with Oxygen Media; plays the role of Sethe in the film *Beloved;* named one of *Time* magazine's 100 Most Influential People of the 20th Century.
2000	Launches *O, The Oprah Magazine,* in April.
2002	Launches first international edition of *O, The Oprah Magazine* in South Africa in April; Harpo Studios produces and syndicates *Dr. Phil,* which debuts on September 16; The Oprah Winfrey Foundation initiates ChristmasKindness in South Africa 2002.
2003	Launches largest book club in the world through Oprah.com.
2004	Renews contract for *The Oprah Winfrey Show* through the 2010-2011 season; debuts *O At Home.*
2005	Named one of *Time* magazine's 100 Most Influential People in the World; named number one on *Forbes*'s Power Celebrity 100 list; becomes the first black person listed by *BusinessWeek* as one of America's top fifty most generous philanthropists.

2006 Produces talk show hosted by Rachael Ray;
with Harpo Radio, Inc. and XM Satellite Radio,
launches *Oprah & Friends*.

2007 Opens the Oprah Winfrey Leadership Academy
for Girls in South Africa.

2008 Announces creation of OWN, the Oprah Winfrey
Network with Discovery Communications.

Sources

CHAPTER ONE: "The Talkingest Child"

p. 11, "[People] would say to my grandmother . . ."
"Celebrity Central: Oprah Winfrey," *People*, http://
www.people.com/people/oprah_winfrey/biography.

p. 15-16, "I started out speaking . . ." "Building a Dream:
The Chance of a Lifetime," Oprah.com, http://www.
oprah.com/presents/2007/academy/girls/interviews_
110.jhtml.

p. 16, "I had no relationship . . ." Henry Louis Gates
Jr., *Finding Oprah's Roots* (New York: Crown
Publishers, 2007), 49.

p. 16, "I instantly knew that . . ." Gates, *Finding
Oprah's Roots*, 50.

p. 17, "My grandmother really raised me . . ." Ibid.

p. 17, "Dear Miss Newe, I do not . . ." Oprah Winfrey,
"The Best of Oprah's What I Know for Sure," *O, The
Oprah Magazine*, September 2000, 10.

p. 18, "She so believed in me . . ." "National Teacher
Day 2007: Celebrities, Notable Public Figures Reveal
Their Most Memorable Teachers," National Educational

Association Web site, http://www.nea.org/teacherday/
celebrity.html.

p. 18, "Come live with me . . ." Bill Adler, ed., *The
Uncommon Wisdom of Oprah Winfrey: A Portrait in
Her Own Words* (Secaucus, N.J: Birch Lane Press,
1997), 10.

p. 18, "That whole part of my life . . ." Gates, *Finding
Oprah's Roots,* 51-52.

p. 19, "I didn't tell anybody . . ." George Mair, *Oprah
Winfrey: The Real Story* (New York: Carl Publishing
Group, 1994), 14.

p. 19, "a sexually promiscuous teenager." Gates,
Finding Oprah's Roots, 56.

p. 20, "The life that I saw . . ." Mair, *Oprah Winfrey:
The Real Story*, 17-18.

p. 21, "I was so ashamed . . . Ginger Adams Otis,
"Oprah's Painful Years," *New York Post*, May 27, 2007.

p. 21, "I went back to school . . ." Gates, *Finding
Oprah's Roots*, 58.

p. 21, "What you have done . . ." Otis, "Oprah's
Painful Years."

p. 21-22, "That was the first time . . ." Gates, *Finding
Oprah's Roots*, 42.

p. 23, "I used to do them for churches . . ." "Oprah
Winfrey Interview," Academy of Achievement
Web site, February 21, 1991, http://www.achievement.
org/autodoc/page/win0int-1.

p. 27, "I had to work after school . . ." Ibid.

P. 27, "I made this big speech . . ." Ibid.

CHAPTER TWO: "This Is What I Should Have Been Doing"

p. 29, "I'd never even been behind the scenes . . ." "Oprah Winfrey Interview," Academy of Achievement Web site.

p. 30, "So I decided to pretend to be . . ." Ibid.

p. 30, "So I'd do all my classes in the morning . . ." Ibid.

p. 32, "I used to go on assignment . . ." Ibid.

p. 32, "I only came to co-host . . ."Ibid.

p. 34, "And I'm telling you . . ." Ibid.

p. 36, "When you have finished growing . . ." Mair, *Oprah Winfrey: The Real Story*, 53.

p. 38, "You should go to Chicago . . ." Oprah Winfrey, "The Best of Oprah's What I Know for Sure," *O, The Oprah Magazine*, August 2001, 34.

p. 38, "I'll tell you this . . ." Mair, *Oprah Winfrey: The Real Story*, 73.

CHAPTER THREE: *The Oprah Winfrey Show*

p. 42, "What [Oprah] lacks in journalistic toughness . . ." Richard Zoglin, "Lady with a Calling," *Time*, August 8, 1988.

p. 44 "I thought of *The Color Purple* . . ." "Oprah Winfrey Interview," Academy of Achievement Web site.

p. 44, "the single happiest day . . ." Mair, *Oprah Winfrey: The Real Story*, 86.

p. 45, "I felt at the time . . ." "Oprah Winfrey Interview," Academy of Achievement Web site.

p. 45, "[S]he said, 'You just dream. . .'" Ibid.

p. 47, "Let's talk about the issue . . . you're not the only one," Jack Mathews, "3 'Color Purple' Actresses Talk About Its Impact," *Los Angeles Times*, January 31, 1986.

CHAPTER FOUR: "You Could Own Your Own Show"

p. 49, "I intend to do . . ." Mair, *Oprah Winfrey: The Real Story*, 94.

p. 51, "[Winfrey is] quality, she's got a quality show . . ." Steve Lohr, "Roger M. King, 63, TV Syndicator, Dies," *New York Times*, December 10, 2007.

p. 52, "colorful, controversial, and soaring . . ." Mair, *Oprah Winfrey: The Real Story*, 100.

p. 54, "He says, 'You can own your own show . . ." "Oprah Winfrey Interview," Academy of Achievement Web site.

p. 54, "[T]he studio came about . . ." Ibid.

p. 57, "a story of broken dreams . . ." Mair, *Oprah Winfrey: The Real Story*, 162.

p. 57, "maintaining your dignity in . . ." Ibid.

p. 57, "He's kind, and he's supportive . . ." "Celebrity Central: Oprah Winfrey, *People* Web site.

CHAPTER FIVE: Finding Herself, Helping Others

p. 61-62, "My family, like thousands of others . . ." Adler, *The Uncommon Wisdom of Oprah Winfrey*, 266.

p. 62, "committed to empowering women . . ." Michelle Conlin, "A Talk with Oprah Winfrey, *Business Week*, November 29, 2004.

p. 62, "we have awarded hundreds of grants . . ." Ibid.

p. 62, "I don't think you ever . . ." "Oprah Winfrey Interview," Academy of Achievement Web site.

p. 64, "I think it was on that day . . ." Ibid.

p. 64, "I thought I was going . . ." Ibid.

p. 64-65, "A part of my mission . . ." Ibid.

p. 66, "[T]here are no children here . . ." Alexx Kotlowitz, *There Are No Children Here: The Story of Two Boys Growing Up in the Other America* (New York: Anchor, 1992).

p. 67, "Black people are not . . ." John O'Connor, "Review/Television; Diverse Young Voices Speak on Racism," *New York Times*, January 28, 1993.

p. 67, "My greatest failure . . ." "Celebrity Central: Oprah Winfrey," *People* magazine online.

CHAPTER SIX: A Positive Message

p. 73, "I am embarrassed by how . . ." Oprah Winfrey, "What We All Can Do to Change TV," *TV Guide*, November 11, 1995, 15-16.

p. 75, "1. Life is a journey . . ." Pat and Ruth Williams, *How to Be Like Women of Influence* (Deerfield Beach, Fla.: Health Communications, 2003), 105.

p. 78, "I just expected, oh, it's going . . ." "Oprah Expresses Disappointment Over Beloved," *Movie/TV News*, May 12, 1999, http://imdb.com/news/sb/1999-05-12#film6.

p. 79-80, "[M]y intention is always . . ." "Oprah Winfrey Interview," Academy of Achievement Web site.

p. 80, "just stopped me cold . . ." "Oprah Accused of Whipping Up Anti-Beef 'Lynch Mob,'" CNN Interactive, January 21, 1998, http://www.cnn.com/US/9801/21/oprah.beef/.

CHAPTER SEVEN: Adding to the O Empire

p. 85, "personal-growth manual," Patricia Sellers, "The Business of Being Oprah," *Fortune*, April 1, 2002.

p. 85, "I wasn't too controlling . . ." Lynette Clemetson, "It Is Constant Work," *Newsweek,* January 8, 2001.

p. 85-86, "She's into every little niggly thing . . ." Sellers, "The Business of Being Oprah."

p. 87, "It was [Oprah's] vision . . ." *Television Week,* April 19, 2004, S4.

p. 89-90, "My life was dramatically . . ." "What Is ChristmasKindness"? http://www. oprah.com/video/presents/ck/ck_/clip_1_qxx_f.jhtml.

p. 91, "What I wanted to do . . ." Oprah Winfrey, "Statement from Oprah Winfrey," *Boston.com*, January 20, 2007, http://www.boston.com/news/world/africa/articles/2007/01/20/statement_from_oprah_winfrey/.

p. 91-92, "It's my vision . . ." Conlin, "A Talk with Oprah Winfrey."

p. 92, "From the very beginning of designing . . ." Oprah Winfrey, "Statement from Oprah Winfrey," Boston.com, January 20, 2007.

p. 92-93, "When I first started making . . ." Allison Samuels, "Oprah Goes to School," *Newsweek*, January 8, 2007.

CHAPTER EIGHT: The Oprah Legacy

p. 99, "These women, who have . . ." Aldore D. Collier, "Oprah Honors Her Heroes at Three-Day Bash in Santa Barbara, CA," *Jet*, June 6, 2005.

p. 99, "Oprah told me this has . . ." William Keck, "Winfrey Hosts 'A Love Fest," *USA Today*, May 15, 2005.

p. 102, "did not reflect my voice . . .of the channel," Frank Ahrens, "Discovery, Winfrey to Team Up on Network," *Washington Post*, January 16, 2008.

p. 102, "entertain, inform and inspire . . ." Discovery Communications Web site "Special Announcement: Oprah Winfrey and Discovery Communications to Form New Joint Venture," January 15, 2008, http://corporate.discovery.com/news/press/08q1/announcement_0115.html.

p. 102, "vision of creating . . ." Phil Rosenthal, "Winfrey to Start Own TV Network," *Chicago Tribune*, January 16, 2008.

p. 102, "Fifteen years ago, I wrote . . ." Discovery Communications Web site "Special Announcement," January 15, 2008.

p. 103, "The truth of the matter is..." Phil Rosenthal, "Winfrey to Start Own TV Network."

p. 103, "There's no stronger brand . . ." Ibid.

p. 103, "Everybody's thinking, 'I gotta get . . ." Sellers, "The Business of Being Oprah."

p. 103, "If I lost control of the business . . ." Ibid.

p. 104. "You wouldn't say . . ." Ibid.

p. 106, "Education is freedom. It provides . . ."

Conlin, "A Talk with Oprah Winfrey.

p. 107, "I became so frustrated . . ." Ibid.

p. 108, "I think that all crisis is there . . ." Jeb Dreben, "Oprah Winfrey: 'I Don't Regret' Opening School," December 12, 2007, *People* Web site, http://www. people.com/people/article/0,,20165725,00.html.

p. 108, "I think that what [Obama] stands for . . ." Juston Jones, "When It Comes to Politics, Friendship Has Its Limits," *New York Times,* July 23, 2007.

p. 108, "Making other people happy..." Conlin, "A Talk with Oprah Winfrey."

Bibliography

Adler, Bill, ed. *The Uncommon Wisdom of Oprah Winfrey: A Portrait in Her Own Words.* Secaucus, N.J: Birch Lane Press, 1997.

Anderson, Chris. "Meet Oprah Winfrey." *Good Housekeeping,* August 1986.

Bosman, Julie. "Celebrity Power; The Oprah Factor and Obama." *New York Times,* September 11, 2007.

Carr, David. "Oprah Puts Her Brand on the Line." *New York Times,* December 24, 2007.

Clemetson, Lynette. "It Is Constant Work." *Newsweek,* January 8, 2001.

Conlin, Michelle. "A Talk with Oprah Winfrey." *Business Week,* November 29, 2004.

Corliss, Richard. "Bewitching Beloved." *Time,* October 5, 1998.

Dedman, Bill. "Personal Business: Professor Oprah, Preaching What She Practices." *New York Times,* October 10, 1999.

Dreben, Jeb. "Oprah Winfrey: 'I Don't Regret' Opening School." *People,* December 12, 2007.

Friedman, Roger. "Oprah Winfrey's Charities Worth More Than $200 Million." *FoxNews.com,* January 5, 2007. http:

//www.foxnews.com/story/0,2933,241782,00.html.

Garson, Helen S. *Oprah Winfrey: A Biography.* Westport: Conn.: Greenwood Press, 2004.

Gates, Henry Louis Jr. *Finding Oprah's Roots: Finding Your Own.* New York: Crown Publishers, 2007.

Harrison, Barbara Grizzuti. "The Importance of Being Oprah." *New York Times Magazine*, June 11, 1989.

Jones, Juston. "When It Comes to Politics, Friendship Has Its Limits." *New York Times,* July 23, 2007.

Lawrence, Ken. *The World According to Oprah.* Kansas City: Andrews McMeel, 2005.

Levenson, Eugenia. "Hall of Fame." *Fortune*, November 14, 2005.

Mair, George. *Oprah Winfrey: The Real Story.* New York: Carl Publishing Group, 1994.

Matthews, Jack. "3 'Color Purple' Actresses Talk About Its Impact." *Los Angeles Times*, January 31, 1986.

Oldenburg, Ann. "The Divine Miss Winfrey?" *USA Today*, May 11, 2006.

"Oprah on Oprah." *Newsweek*, January 8, 2001.

Otis, Ginger Adams. "Oprah's Painful Years." *New York Post*, May 27, 2007.

Richman, Alan. "Oprah." *People,* January 12, 1987.

Rosenthal, Phil. "Winfrey to Start Own TV Network." *Chicago Tribune,* January 16, 2008.

Sellers, Patricia. "The Business of Being Oprah." *Fortune*, April 1, 2002.

The Showbuzz. "'The Color Purple' Closing on Broadway." January 24, 2008, http://www.showbuzz.cbsnews.com/stories/2008/01/24/ theater/main3749702.shtml.

Silverman, Stephen. "Ex Oprah School Employee Arrested on Abuse Charge." *People,* November 2, 2007.

Tannen, Deborah. "Oprah Winfrey." *Time*, June 8, 1998.

Timberg, Bernard, and Robert J. Erler. *Television Talk: A History of the TV Talk Show.* Austin, Texas: University of Texas Press, 2002.

Waldron, Robert. *Oprah!* New York: St. Martin's Press, 1987.

"Why Oprah Opens Readers' Wallets." *BusinessWeek,* October 10, 2005.

Winfrey, Oprah. "Graduation Address." Wesleyan University, Middletown, Connecticut, May 1998.

———. "What We All Can Do to Change TV." *TV Guide,* November 11, 1995.

———. Winfrey, Oprah. "The Best of Oprah's What I Know For Sure." *The Oprah Winfrey Magazine.*

Zoglin, Richard. "Lady with a Calling." *Time,* August 8, 1988.

Web sites

http://www.oprah.com/
Oprah Winfrey official site

http://www.achievement.org/autodoc/page/win0int-1
Oprah Winfrey profile at Academy of Achievement

http://oprahwinfreyleadershipacademy.o-philanthropy.
org/site/PageServer?pagename=owla_homepage
Oprah Winfrey: The Leadership Academy for Girls

http://www.biography.com/search/article.do?id=9534419
Oprah Winfrey biography: *Biography* magazine online

http://www.oprah.com/omagazine/omag_landing.jhtml
O, The Oprah Magazine

http://www.oprah.com/presents/2006/legends/legends_
main.jhtml
Oprah's Legends Weekend

http://www.museum.tv/archives/etv/W/htmlW/winfreyo-
pra/winfreyopra.htm
The Museum of Broadcast Communications: Winfrey, Oprah:
U.S. Talk Show Host

http://www.referenceforbusiness.com
An online encyclopedia that features biographies of business leaders as well as company profiles. An Oprah biography appears on the site as well as information about Harpo, Inc.

Index